I. BURNS

the Basic Arts of Management

the
Basic Arts of Management

W. J. TAYLOR   T. F. WATLING

Foreword by
THE RT HON RICHARD MARSH

Business Books Limited   London

First published 1972
Second Impression 1972

ISBN 0 220 66812 4

By the same authors:
Successful Project Management
Business Books

This book has been set in 10 on 11 pt. Times Roman:
printed in England by Clarke, Doble & Brendon Ltd, Plymouth
for the publishers, Business Books Limited (registered
office: 180 Fleet Street, London, E.C.4),
publishing offices: Mercury House, Waterloo Road, London, S.E.1

MADE AND PRINTED IN GREAT BRITAIN

Contents

Acknowledgements

The authors wish to thank ICL for allowing them to have the book published and for the helpful comments of colleagues Mr N. D. Hill, Mr J. R. Cartwright, Mr A. McG. Leckie and Mr A. D. Rymell. A special thanks goes to Miss Carole Duggan for typing and secretarial services.

Foreword

The book is intended to provide a sound introduction to management for the younger manager and could, with advantage, be studied by many older managers for its restatement of basic principles. It emphasises the importance of the basic arts of management and shows that although there are many attempts to slice a new piece of scientific cake from the job the basic arts remain the same.

The book has no industry bounds and is equally applicable to management in a large nationalised industry, such as the railways, as to a small company. Stress is laid on the theme that any manager can fill his day with work of some kind but only a small proportion of his effort should go to routine tasks. Effective management becomes much easier when a manager understands the ground rules. He can then concentrate on the real issue of the moment.

The authors are project managers and as such have included a chapter on the subject. It is wise for managers to understand the differences and similarities between line management and project management.

This book is a useful contribution to wider understanding of what management entails and, therefore, to greater efficiency. It also has the somewhat unusual characteristic for a book on management that it is readable.

The Rt. Hon. Richard Marsh

Chairman, British Railways Board

Introduction

Our intention in writing this book is to provide a straightforward introduction to management. We feel that too often people are thrust into their first management job with no preparation at all. They are faced with many practical problems which can be worrying to those without previous experience. We have set out to try to give some practical guidance to new managers and, we hope, greater effectiveness to experienced ones.

There is a lot of talk about what makes a good manager. The one expression which crops up repeatedly is that a manager must be a 'self-starter'. We believe that a manager sets out with a positive approach. He sets himself targets of performance and goes all out to achieve them. Managers think and plan but above all effective managers get things done. Every time a manager opens his mouth to blame 'them' for some shortcoming, he should ask himself 'Can I do anything about it?'

The majority of managers coast along. No one is likely to stop you if you take on work and do it effectively, unless your company is so grossly over-staffed that everyone is defending their own area. Most senior managers welcome the subordinate who is prepared to take work off their shoulders: yours is likely to be the same. Take on small jobs first and prove you can do them. Once people know you are effective and can get things done, then the interesting jobs will start to come your way. This is the way to broaden your experience and start to climb the management ladder.

In your early days as a new manager you may have to go to your own manager for help and advice. When you have to go to him with a problem, try to go not just with the problem but also with a solution.

The most important aspect of your job as a new manager is dealing with people and we have consequently given over a large part of this book to the manager and people. Personnel managers have a tendency to treat people as units and fit them all into little square pigeon holes. Real people don't all have nice square heads to fit into nice square pigeon holes. Line managers must see their people as people and get good results from round heads as well as square heads. They must also get results from the awkward ones, whose heads are of no easily defined geometric shape. People are of primary importance to managers. People also have a knack of seeing their manager as he really is. You may be able to fool your own manager some of the time, to flannel him or blind him with science. However, it is quite certain you will not fool the people who work for you. They recognise quite quickly the manager of integrity. To obtain the confidence of the people who work for him is the first task of a manager.

You may sometimes be told 'We always do it this way' or 'We've never done it like this before.' These expressions clearly define a rut which should be avoided. There may well be good reasons for the existing way of doing things but the mere fact that 'we've always done it this way' is most emphatically not a good reason.

We have said that the effective manager is one who gets things done. An absolute prerequisite for getting things done is for you always to know clearly what you are setting out to do and have an absolute determination to do it. Determination is not something we can teach you; you either have it in yourself or you haven't. A man who can summon little determination is not likely to make a good manager. It is not sufficient, of course, just to get things done but to set out to do them at the right time, at the right cost and so that the end result is correct.

If you have the determination to succeed in management, then one of the first areas to which you must give attention is management of yourself. As a manager you are expected to plan your own work. You will no longer be subject to detailed supervision. You will be judged on the results you achieve.

In Part One (Chapters 1 to 6), we deal with managing yourself and we start with the use of your time. We all know the man who spends so much time telling people how busy he is that he can't ever get anything done. We will show you how to use your time effectively to achieve results.

If you are to do a good job you must know what your job really is. We show you how to identify the real job. Most of us have ambitions for the future. We discuss how to achieve your ambitions. We discuss the routine affairs of running your own office and we discuss the problems involved in decision making.

In Part Two (Chapters 7 to 12), we go on to the all important subject of managing people. How do you get people to work for you? Not just to put in the hours but to achieve effective results? The secret lies in setting people free to perform. We go on from this to discuss the need to reward people, not just because we like them but because they produce results.

One subject of crucial importance to the new manager is the problem and also opportunity of taking over existing staff. After this we discuss the recruitment of new staff, possibly one of the greatest opportunities any manager has to influence the future of his organisation.

Communication of ideas is crucial to modern managers. Ideas have to be conveyed to your staff, your seniors, your colleagues, suppliers and customers. We cannot overstress the importance of this subject. Communication is essentially a two way affair. We must not forget that we are on the receiving end as well.

The final chapter in this part considers organisation. A partnership of two or three people may work without any formal organisation. This may possibly work well because they know each other very well and have informally, perhaps without even being conscious of it, divided the work between them. Companies with twenty people upwards find it difficult to function without some formal organisation pattern. Chapter 12 forms an introduction to the subjects.

Perhaps the most important subject to a manager, after people, is money. We devote Part Three of the book to this. First, as an introduction, we deal with some personal money considerations of interest to the manager as an individual. We go on to introduce budgets, company finance and the subject of financial choice of projects. The end chapter of this part is devoted to value for money.

We've called the last part of our book 'Be in Front: Keep in Front.' A manager is not alone in his work. The experience of many people is enshrined in various techniques, which are available to any manager who cares to learn about them. Project management techniques, for example, can be particularly useful and we have devoted a chapter to this subject. This is followed by a chapter introducing some further management techniques.

No manager in the nineteen-seventies can ignore computers, nor should he. Computers can help managers and we have devoted a chapter to explaining them in simple terms.

Lastly, no company exists solely for its own sake. It is there to make a profit. In the long term it will only make a profit if it fills the needs of the market. So our final chapter is devoted to marketing.

We believe that effective management can be learnt and we have set out in this book to show how you can become an effective manager.

part one Managing Yourself

one Be Effective—Be Successful

To be successful we must be effective. We must have the drive to succeed; we must learn the basic rules of effectiveness. Look around at successful people you know or that you read about in business, sport or commerce, and you will find that in all cases, although some may apparently have inbuilt gifts, all got to where they are by learning to be effective at the thing they do. Practice makes perfect is an old adage. It is just as applicable to the effective manager as to any other person. We take it for granted that a footballer, boxer, runner or pianist has to practise over and over again to become the effective practitioner of his sport or profession. Strangely enough many people have the total misconception that to be a manager one just needs a room, a carpet on the floor and a name on the door. It is possible, of course, for some form of management to be carried out by virtually anybody, but here we are not concerned with just managing something, but with managing effectively. We will illustrate the differences between effective and non-effective managers. What we can't give you is your own *determination to succeed*.

First we need a simple general description of effectiveness that is clear and unambiguous. It is: *The measure of effectiveness is how well a manager achieves the agreed objectives of his position. This is his real task.*

Note that it is not what he is, or what he does, but *what he achieves*, e.g.

What I am	Manager of a small sales force
What I do	Sell products X and Y

What I must achieve *The expansion of sales of products X and Y by 10 per cent this year without increasing my resources*

An insurance friend of ours when talking about this achievement question said 'I could simply say I am an area manager and I look after six salesmen, but I know my real job is to plan ahead, encourage and guide my men so that we all meet our targets with the amount of insurance actually sold. I'm lucky, we not only have the targets, but also the incentive that every £1000 sold means an addition to my pension. Not everyone has these dual goals to strive for.'

Manufacturing managers have achievements in mind when they say 'It's not only so many units produced per year but ensuring that targets of timescale, cost, quality and reliability are met as well. Then we can say we are really making objective achievements to the benefit of our company.'

Some of you may say that in your particular job it is too difficult to set objectives, and hence measure achievements. Some jobs are difficult, especially if the end result cannot be measured in so many output units, but they are never impossible to specify. In some way too your achievement must come through simply by making people sit up and notice that when you are around something of benefit to your company gets done. Whatever your job, think: what can I do that really benefits my company, however small it may be, something that will add to its overall achievements? Remember, only the 'What I must achieve' is meaningful in terms of effective management.

EFFICIENCY VERSUS EFFECTIVENESS

Efficiency is not necessarily synonymous with effectiveness. An engineering manager we know has the most untidy desk you can imagine. His filing system appears chaotic. His secretary long ago abandoned any hope of reforming him into tidiness. Yet he is an acknowledged expert at his job. He looks ahead; he initiates projects which are profitable and he is ruthless in cutting out unnecessary and costly refinements and design complications. He gets things done on time, to the required performance standards and at the agreed level of costs. In short, he is an effective manager. The administrators calling for returns and trying to enforce petty rules find him a trial. They regard his untidy office as an eyesore and would rate him as inefficient. His company's senior management put great value on his services because they see beyond the surface inefficiencies to the results he gets. We do not advocate sloppy administration and untidiness, but do not confuse tidy conformity with effectiveness.

In one company we visited we were shown with great pride the invoicing department. The area shone with neatness and cleanliness. The manager talked to us and was obviously proud of his apparently efficient department of some 40 invoicing clerks. We asked him about his staff and he told us that he increased them by about 15 per cent each year, 'To cope with the additional business you know.' We then asked what his objectives were in the department and his reply was 'Obviously prepare the invoices.' We went on questioning him but at no time did he mention what he might be trying to achieve, only the work he did.

Another manager might have said 'There are 40 clerks here and this puts certain overheads on each invoice. What I must find out are ways of achieving the invoicing at less cost while still maintaining the quality and accuracy of the work.' He then might have gone on to talk of looking at more automatic means, a small computer maybe, if its cost could be justified, or any new methods of dealing with his work in order to achieve more to benefit his company. In this example it is also clear that higher management were not being very effective in allowing such a state of affairs to persist.

The Basic Rules

Once you have made the decision that you are going to succeed in management then the next job is to learn the basic rules. First and foremost must come the management of yourself. Peter Drucker has said 'Unless he (the executive) manages himself effectively no amount of abiliity, skill, experience or knowledge will make him an effective executive.' Effective management is far more than just managing the work of others. Like many other professions it consists of a system of disciplines which when learnt thoroughly and practised assiduously will fit most people for a higher level than that in which they now find themselves. Effective management, therefore, can be learned. We must learn to concentrate on essentials.

QUITE RUTHLESSLY REMOVING ALL THE
DEADWOOD IN YOUR JOB

You know the sort of deadwood that gathers in a management job: unnecessary correspondence, unnecessary meetings, jobs

7

which your staff can do just as well as you, perhaps better, minor decisions that someone else could take and a thousand and one other unnecessary time wasters. By learning how to see the wood from the trees we are most likely to be able to see, for example, the advantages of technological change and exploit the opportunities that could arise.

In the deadwood also comes the work that will no longer be productive: the project that is not going to achieve anything for the company, no experience, no profit or making too low a profit. Our expectations of projects change over time. The most carefully planned ones sometimes have to be killed in order to release resources for a more profitable project. We have to recognise these projects and clear them away like the deadwood they are. One managing director when asked about this said 'One of the big weaknesses in many managers is carrying on with jobs that will clearly not help the company results. Like the shopkeeper, we must clear out the non-productive lines.'

KNOWING HOW TO SPEND YOUR TIME

We shall tell you much more about time and how to use it, but the important thing to know now is that the maximum time must be used in the really important jobs. It is only too easy to fritter time away on unimportant matters. We all know the sound of the grasshopper man as he jumps from job to job crying 'I'm so busy I haven't time to do my job properly.' Probably the most important lesson we can learn concerning time is that the greatest benefit occurs when time is brought in the 'giant' size economy package.

DO WELL THE JOBS YOU DECIDE TO DO

If you use your time correctly you will pick out the key jobs and you must do them well. Success does not come from running every race, it comes from winning the races you enter. In learning how to do a few jobs properly, we ought to widen our general business knowledge in order that our business acumen and entrepreneurial flair has a chance to grow.

MAKE EFFECTIVE DECISIONS

Decisions have to mean something. You have heard the man who boasts that he always makes a decision, and quickly. While decisions are of course very important and necessary, in many cases they either do not need to be made rashly or the right decision

8

may be to consider whether the question was right, not just to answer it. We need to learn, however, how to make short-term tactical decisions without hindering long-term strategic considerations.

MANAGEMENT INNOVATION

That is rather a grand title for making sure that you keep some time for thinking about new ideas and testing them out in your job. We must develop the ability to introduce new methods. This involves the company through from ideas into effective action. It requires the ability to persuade other people to adopt your ideas.

Planning for Effectiveness

Like any other task the system of effective management requires a plan to make it happen. The planning is largely by 'management by objectives'. This simply means that the objectives of any managerial task are stated in advance. They are agreed objectives in that the manager concerned agrees them in advance with his own senior manager. We then finish up with the company having throughout a complete corporate plan and agreed objectives with all managers. This does not mean that managers are then in a straitjacket, but throughout the company there now exists targets for all to strive for. This gives the best chance of success and makes managers grow in skills.

The total plan is formulated by the company in the light of past achievements and what the company hopes to do in the future. While the subject of corporate planning is not within the scope of this book the most important thing to be said about it is that plans must exist for turnover, profit, expenditure, manpower, product development, etc, for up to 5 years in the majority of businesses. In others the planning may extend to 10 or 15 years. The planning will be on a continuous basis, updated every year. More or less irrevocable commitment of expenditure on plant and materials may have to take place up to 2 years before delivery, but every year there will be a new look at the plan and adjustments will be made. As a manager each one of us has some part to play in setting the overall targets for our company and setting out to achieve or better them.

THE MANAGER'S OBJECTIVES

The objectives agreed must be hard enough to make the manager grow in his abilities, but they must not be impossible. Inbuilt into them are other factors as well as the value of sales which must be achieved, how many units must be produced or other measure of achievement. These factors are also essential to the effectiveness of the manager:

1 FREEDOM TO PERFORM The manager must be allowed to do the job in his own way. He knows what he has to achieve; he must be allowed to do it. The resources he needs to meet his objectives will have been broadly agreed beforehand.

2 ASSESSMENT AND GUIDANCE The manager's performance must be assessed on how far he achieves his objectives. Guidance must be given to him if necessary. This must be done without interfering with his freedom to perform.

3 TRAINING This must be provided both by the proper job succession, and any specialised training necessary. It is sensible that the company do all they can to fit the manager for his task. This must be part of the 'company objectives'.

4 REWARD AND PROMOTION This is both part of the job succession plan and individual reward for performance achievements. Rewards must be given to those who deserve them, not shared with the non-performers, otherwise incentive is lost and merit goes unrewarded.

two Your Time: Use it, not Abuse it!

Introduction

Years—70—80—90 years—maybe 100 or more; averages, statistics, actuaries. Expressions like these come into 'years of life' for all of us. A great part of this time is spent at work and, for most of us, earning money. To appreciate what we do with our time we need to take a close look at a bit of it that makes up our life. Let us choose a day, since it is a complete unit. We work, eat and sleep, all in one day.

Is there any difference between your day and anyone else's day? The first reaction perhaps is about what each does in the day, and the answer would be yes, there must be a difference. One thing, however, is the same, and we can start from this fundamental premise. Each of us has in each day 1440 minutes, no more and no less. At the end of the day they are gone, never to return. But, we may argue, there is another day. There is another, but not this one that has just gone. This is the first and most important realisation that we must all come to accept. There will not be another day to make up for today, whether it has been good, bad or indifferent.

This does not mean we all have to rush into nervous hysteria to try to account for every one of these precious minutes. Not at all. What it does mean is that we must become more conscious of time in a way we did not consider before. Once we have achieved this real consciousness of time and what we do with it, or, more important, what we *can* do with it, we are able to take the next step in the management of our own time.

11

Work

Work consists of a mixture of jobs. Some must be done today, some can, or must, wait; some are not really jobs at all; some are expected, some unexpected; some pleasant and some boring or unpleasant. Some jobs will take more than a day, some less. There are subdivisions *ad nauseam*.

How do we set about deciding what to do in a day? As managers we are expected in varying degrees to make this choice for ourselves. There can be a bewildering lot of possibilities, all apparently wanted at once. Do we see Mr Evans who wants to talk to us urgently about a personal problem? Do we get out with a salesman who wants help on a new contract? Do we write the report that our manager is requesting as urgent? Do we get down to concentrate on a technical problem? When can we clear that mounting mail in the in-tray? What do we do?

Firstly we have to train ourselves so that we are not conscious of a mass of jobs waiting to be done. This is not easy to begin with, but there is a method to get on top of work. Use time properly, all 1440 minutes of it each day. Less sleep, of course, which most authorities on the subject tell us demands 8 hours or 480 minutes. That leaves 960 minutes. (We will come to the eating part later!)

Allocation of Time

It depends, of course, what level of management we are at as to how we may ultimately allocate our time, but at all levels of management certain basic rules apply. The allocation of time does not imply that all jobs have to be included. In fact, the first rule is:

Always take the top few jobs that will benefit everybody most and get them done first. Don't waste the top minutes on minor jobs that either somebody else can do or benefits less the company and its people. It is a generally accepted fact by purchasing personnel that of the parts, roughly 80 per cent of the cost is applied to 20 per cent of the parts by volume. In a similar manner most managers find that only a small percentage, some 10 to 15 per cent, of the tasks are vital and should demand 85 to 90 per cent of the manager's time. The rest can be done in the 10 to 15 per cent time left. Your use of time should be similar. The accent must be on contribution to the good of the company and its staff.

Job Order

What sort of tasks must really come first? As far as ever possible, the main grouping must be:

Your staff.
—Your customers.
—The rest.

These are the broad principles. Sometimes there will be difficulty in adhering to them; it is not a perfect world. Your staff must come first because you need them to make sure your department, and from this your company, is doing the job it was formed to do. This may be sales, research, production or project management, etc. To perform any of these functions demands that your staff are properly paid, housed, trained and treated. It does not mean mollycoddling, but it does mean an intelligent, adult and businesslike relationship. After the broad principles, what about your own more detailed order of doing work? This will become clear when work planning has been dealt with, but there is one general rule in choosing the job order. There will often be tough jobs that demand a great deal of thought and tiring mental effort. Choose the time for these tasks when you are most alert, probably first thing in the morning.

Work Planning

Selecting jobs must not be random. You will need a plan of work. Set yourself targets. Today I will do this! If you do this planning every day for a period ahead, you will acquire capacity for doing more and more work. Here is the next rule then:

Plan your work. Make tight but achievable targets for yourself. Don't let jobs run on. Break up your day into intervals of time that you can fit and measure against individual jobs. Don't allocate time out of proportion to the importance of the job.

When you have done this for a week or two, you will gradually appreciate that you are doing much more real work than you used to.

It is interesting to watch ourselves and others planning instinctively the steps in, say, catching a long-distance train or plane. Most people though not all, we admit, will immediately formulate a plan. Arrive a little before needed, allow time to get to the station, fix the time to leave home or office. Invariably we keep

13

to these timetables. Bring the same disciplines to bear in work planning. In your planning you must leave some time for contingencies and also arrange for standby or fill-in jobs so that if you do better than your planned work you can fill in with some more. Likewise, if contingencies don't arise you can fill in.

Here is a very common contingency:

If you have callers that are not on today's schedule, weigh the importance of their call against today's time. Never be rude, always polite. Listen and talk interestedly and be helpful, but do not settle in your chair if you want the visit really short. Standing up for a while will probably do you good anyway.

Two more general rules:

Unless there are good sound reasons to delay (and that does not mean just because you want to delay) do it now! Don't put off until tomorrow what you can do today. That old adage is absolutely right. Don't lose any of those 960 minutes that comprise today.

Finish one job before starting another. Don't grasshopper around on several jobs. None will get done properly.

Finally:

Include in your plan of work time to think about your next plan of work. Also time to think about activities to benefit the company and its staff.

Finding More Time

This sounds a bit of a contradiction in terms since we've already been at pains to say there are only 960 available minutes in the day. Of course, you can't find more time in the absolute sense, but you can do three things to make more time for work.

WORK LONGER HOURS?

Within reason for most people, yes! Try starting work a bit earlier instead of falling through the office door at 9 a.m. Quarter hour, half hour, one hour? Try half an hour for a start. You can easily vary it afterwards. It's amazing what that quiet half hour can do. Use it for the hard ones when quiet thought and hard concentration are essential.

As well as an early start, what about the other end of the day?

14

A few extra minutes to finish up before the next day can work wonders.

You must decide for yourself how much extra time you either wish to or can work. Some men or women will work all the hours they can in an endeavour to reach the pinnacle of their ambitions. A large number of people like to do extra time in moderation. Extra time does a lot towards work enhancement but for most people it will be in moderation and the timings varied.

DELEGATE

Let others do some of the work. There are triple advantages from delegating. You have more time to do your job, and some more delegated from your boss. You are providing training and opportunities for other people. You are preparing yourself for promotion.

One of the enemies of delegation is the apparently logical attitude that it sometimes takes longer to tell someone what to do than it takes to do the job. This is a fatal trap with no escape, for it gets worse on each occasion. Delegate now!

The third way to make more time is much more subtle, much more difficult to achieve, but gives great rewards. It's a tuning up process. *It's more work in the same time.*

There are certain basic aids you can cultivate. Give yourself a week or two to get these aids going for you and think back to what you used to do. Twenty, 30 or 40 per cent plus improvements are common.

READING

Learn to read faster. Try to double your reading speed. Take a short course on it if you want to. You will ultimately find you can read faster and lose nothing of the meaning of what you are reading. You will also remember it just as well. Think what double reading speed could mean over a month or two. In this complex, but fascinating world, there are always plenty of memos, letters, reports, articles and books to read. Read twice as many.

Learn to recognise quickly the material that only needs a cursory glance. Don't waste time by unnecessarily thorough reading and poring over such material.

TALKING

It would be a peculiar existence if nobody talked, but maybe some

15

of us talk too much. While we talk it's doubtful if we can really concentrate on much else. Don't be taciturn, but be economical in talking. That does not mean be uninteresting, it means just saying what we have to say in a minimum of words without, of course, missing out the essential English. Often it can just be the avoidance of repetition. If you think about talking time when you talk, the economy will follow.

The telephone is a great invention, but also a great tempter. The temptation to go on and on is compelling. Don't be tempted! Don't forget that if you talk unnecessarily there are three things happening:

The caller is wasting time and money.

The person at the other end is wasting time.

A telephone line is tied up and perhaps stops someone else from communicating important news of one sort or another.

WRITING

This is a great area for saving time. Make business letters and memos short and to the point. For example:

NOT   We enclose the form No. 203 which we should be glad if you would kindly sign on the dotted line and return as soon as convenient to you so that we can investigate the claim you are making. If it proves satisfactory we shall be pleased to forward you a cheque in due course.

BUT   Please sign and return the enclosed form. Your claim will be investigated quickly and if agreed it will be paid.

There is no doubt the example could be further improved, but there is no need to go beyond the sensible pruning stage. Going further can make a message too terse or too cold. This is not good for communication in general. If work is put into saving time and effort in writing, then there are two important results. First the time of the person receiving the letter is saved and often the message is less ambiguous. Second, more communication takes place because, say, 10 notes can be written instead of 5. This assumes the basic need to write many memos anyway.

If the circumstances permit, an even greater saving can be achieved by avoiding writing the letter or memo altogether. There are too many in all the companies we know. Why not a quick phone call instead?

One somewhat amusing story we have read, and which we hasten to add is not firm advice, is about a very senior civil servant. He became very frustrated about the amount of paper coming into his in-tray. His practice, therefore, every day was to put half of his incoming mail straight into the out-tray without reading it. He calculated he only got about 10 per cent back for a second go.

In this subject of writing also comes speed. Whatever is done, if it is done faster, then again total output must improve. With secretarial assistance shorthand and dictaphone methods help greatly, but if you handwrite then practise quicker, but legible writing for note taking and memo and letter writing.

A lot of us spend much time on debating about things which happened yesterday or earlier. More often than not nothing can now be done about it. Unless there is a clear lesson to learn from a debate on it, leave the subject alone and concentrate on a worthwhile task today.

Meetings

A lot of time is wasted on meetings: probably half of them are not necessary and probably all take twice as long as they need. Multiply this time by all the people who attend, by the number of meetings held in a year and then take the total salary bill. The size of this bill would probably equal the national debt.

This does not, of course, mean that all meetings are useless, but time must be well spent. Make sure that when you attend a meeting, the following rules will be obeyed:

There must be a clear object.
The people who attend must be capable of dealing with the subject.
The subject must be within the scope of the meeting level and ability.
The agenda and timing must do all it can to ensure a quick successful session.
Your own private rule—gauge the successful chairman in advance—they can make or mar the meetings.

Concentration and the Effect on Job Efficiency

In all the work we do whether it is work for reward, a hobby or social help, the keyword must be concentration. It's all a question

c

of bringing the maximum mental or physical energy to bear at the time on a particular task. It's often not easy at first to know whether enough effort is in fact being concentrated on a task. If an awkward nail has to be hammered and it has to be held to keep it in position, most people will concentrate hard. No prizes for the reason, that they might hit their fingers. Perhaps unfortunately, most of our work has no immediate finger pain to prove lack of concentration.

It's easier to recognise lack of concentration than concentration itself. The dreaming while looking out of the office window, listening to the exciting story of what happened to someone last night, the recounting of a television programme, thinking about the impending holiday and general gossip in the office. All sorts of distractions lose us the concentration whereby we can do a job in 20 minutes instead of 2 hours.

All DIY enthusiasts will surely recognise some of the symptoms in the story of the ardent DIY man. He gets up early with a perfect plan of work. First he will finish papering the ceiling of the room he has been decorating for the last week or two. He will then paint the front door which needs doing badly, and then by about 4 p.m. on the Saturday he will slip out to do some last minute shopping.

What actually happened? He got up at 08.00 a.m., had breakfast by 08.30 a.m. and started papering at 08.40. While papering he noticed that his papering table had a screw missing in one of the hinges. He went off to his shed to get a screw. While there, he remembered he had meant to put a shelf up to keep some flower pots which were in danger of getting broken on the floor. 'Well that won't take long, I'll do that,' he said. The shelf was up by 09.45. 'Oh that's a relief, now I can get through the shed to my lathe and finish off the chair legs I was shaping.'

Chair legs completed by lunch time. Into lunch and suddenly he remembered he had started papering. 'Well after lunch I'll soon finish that.' After lunch hard at work papering. While putting up the next to last piece our friend sees the wall brackets he has recently bought. 'I must see whether they fit.' By 4 p.m. he had fixed two brackets and heard his wife call him to go shopping. The saga goes on and another week has to go by before the ceiling is finished. Lack of concentration? Grasshopping? Lack of planning? Allocation of time?

One more thing about concentration. It can be a great benefit occasionally to work at home if this affords the sort of peace sometimes necessary to work out longer-term plans or items which need undisturbed care and thought.

Education and Training

As a manager you must spare time for education and training—for yourself and your staff. Preparing for work and keeping this preparedness up to date is no different than it is for an athlete to keep in training. Most of us easily recognise the latter's need; not all of us recognise that management and staff have a similar need.

There are many ways of achieving the right education and training and certainly many will be particular to an industry. As far as the manager is concerned, there are several things to do to keep fit in the education and training sense.

Know the general picture in your trade or profession by belonging to a learned society or trade association. Attend the meetings and read the appropriate literature. This gives you the 'feel' for your work environment. It's dangerous to get isolated in your own job as developments outside move faster than you think. Get to know the people in your type of work.

Look around often at new products, in reality and in literature, to get ideas of what similar industries and other industries are producing.

Find time to improve your grasp of your particular job. Get as deep an understanding of the principles of what you are trying to do as you can. Get on to appropriate courses. They can have a double advantage. There is further training and also the chance to meet other people.

Find time for education. This means education in a general sense. A broadening of knowledge in subjects completely unrelated to your work. History, fine arts; such activities will give you pleasure, relaxation and interest. They will in their subtle way make you even fitter mentally to tackle the daily work flow.

Fitness

It's pretty obvious that if a person is unfit he or she cannot work at a desirable pace to make a real impact on his work situation and use his time to the best advantage. There have been exceptions to this in history, for example President F. D. Roosevelt who suffered from partial paralysis, Sir Stafford Cripps who was ill

19

THE BASIC ARTS OF MANAGEMENT

for many years and Lord Nelson who was a sufferer from sea sickness!

However, for most of us another old adage is true, 'You can't burn the candle at both ends'. Enough sleep and proper food are essential. No one can prescribe the very best solution, for we must each find it out for ourselves. It is fairly certain that eating and drinking in moderation are important. If you must smoke, then this too should be controlled as there is little doubt that heavy smoking brings nasty rewards, let alone a lack of fitness. What else do we need? Some fun, some relaxation and forgetting work sometimes, are all essentials to a balanced mind and body.

three What is the Real Job?

What is Your Job?

'What is your job?' Ask any manager that question and see what answer you get. 'I'm in charge of the transport.' 'I run the sales force.' 'I'm the marketing manager.' 'I'm responsible for managing the factory.' 'I have a work force of 500 people under me.' All these people confuse the issue. They emphasise the standing or status of their job or the day-to-day mechanics. The job of any manager is to make a contribution to the performance of his company or organisation. For each managerial job there is a specific contribution which is or should be expected.

The sad fact is that a great many managers are passengers; they come along for the ride. They keep the day-to-day routine going in their particular area of the company. If an unusual situation crops up they try to find out what happened last time and do it again. If there is no precedent they ask someone else what to do, generally their own immediate manager. In other words they pass the buck. Most such managers have not deliberately set out to be passengers. They have grown like this over time. They have not bothered to find out what management is all about and in particular they have not thought through their own job.

Well, what is your job? Why does the company have such a job at all? What contribution can you make in this job to the company's success? What did the man who appointed you expect when he made the appointment? What would happen if neither you nor the job existed? It is salutary to ask yourself all these questions. Indeed it is important that you do consider them carefully in your first few days and weeks in your new job. It is all too easy in these first few weeks to become buried in the routine; to exhaust yourself dealing with trivial matters, which your people could handle quite easily. In these circumstances you are soon too tired to think about the job. The question 'what is my job?' seems foolish. You know what your job is. It is coping with the flood of paper work and day-to-day problems. It is *not*. Your job is more than this.

You may belong to a well organised, well managed company. On appointment the contribution expected from you may have been carefully explained to you. However, it is much more likely that you are sent to 'take over as manager of the blanket section.' In these circumstances one of your most important tasks is to formulate your job aim. Put it down succinctly in writing. Then amplify it into a job specification. It is probably wise to keep the first draft to yourself and to gradually refine and improve it as you talk to your staff, your own manager and your colleagues over the first two or three weeks. Don't take their ideas for gospel. Think it out for yourself. The key question to have at the back of your mind is 'How can I contribute to the success of the company?' When you are reasonably satisfied with the job specification, it is sensible to have it typed out and to discuss it with your manager. At this stage, you have at least told him what you are aiming to do and he has the opportunity to tell you if he thinks you are not on the right lines. He may, of course, not believe in job descriptions or modern management methods. Don't let that worry you. These methods will help you to a better performance and he will recognise the better performance even if he doesn't recognise the way in which it has been achieved.

The 90/10 per cent Factor

As well as establishing your aim and defining your job, you should also consider how you are going to do it. Your in-tray may be piled high each morning and there may be a constant stream of visitors. The truth of the matter is that about 90 per cent of the work would be taken care of whether you were there or not. Some of this 90 per cent is routine which your people would cope with in your absence. Because you are there and it is your job, then it comes to you. Part of the 90 per cent is totally unimportant and it would make no difference to the success of the company if it were never done. The remaining 10 per cent or so is the part which really requires the application of your brains and ability. These are the tricky problems, the policy decisions, the decisions which affect other people and the decisions which cost money. Also there is the need to think about the future, about change and improvement. Ten per cent of your time will be nothing like sufficient to handle the important 10 per cent of your job content. You can of course put in a lot of extra hours in order to make the time. This tends to be self-defeating. You become tired, irritable and think less clearly. Your family life suffers and eventually the standard of your work drops and you end up doing as little in the 10 hours a day as you used to do in $7\frac{1}{2}$ hours. You will have to aim at spending 90 per cent of your time on these key 10 per cent areas of your job, leaving only 10 per cent or so of your time to make sure that the routine day-to-day work is going smoothly.

Because you are only going to spend 10 per cent of your time on the routine does not mean that you don't need to understand it. Power and authority go inevitably to those with the appropriate knowledge, who have the skill and determination to use it. If your people, after a few months, realise that you don't understand the routine of the job and have no intention of learning about it, two things will happen. First some will take advantage of your ignorance to get things past you. This may mean they are doing poor work, claiming unnecessary expenses or overtime or even leaving work undone. Needless to say these things may not be obvious at first but they will certainly be reflected in the results of your section in due time. The second thing which will happen is that an unofficial leader will arise. This is not as dramatic as it sounds, but effectively someone will assume your responsibility for solving problems, which can only be solved by someone who really understands what is happening. The rest of the staff will turn to this unofficial leader for help and guidance; people from outside the section will begin to go to him rather than to you with tricky points on which they need guidance. In effect the unofficial leader will gradually usurp your job as manager.

Studying the Work of Your People

Your first few weeks in the new job will very largely be taken up by getting to know your people, trying to define your job and just keeping the job going. However, an appreciable chunk of time in the early weeks and months must be given over to getting a really thorough grasp of the work of the section if, that is, you do not already know it.

This can be approached quite simply. Providing you take time and are methodical about it, there need be no real difficulty. Apart from your pocket notebook, keep an exercise book in which you build up your notes about the job of your section. Build up notes on the structure or organisation of the section and what each man in the section does. This can be done fairly quickly. At the same time try to build a framework into which each man's work fits. Ask the questions: Where does the section's work come from? In what form does it arrive? What essential processing or recording has to be done within the section? What is the end result of the work of the section and where does it go? Finally, why is this work being done and what contribution is it making to the success of the company?

The section's work may come from outside the firm; from customers, suppliers, shareholders or other outside agencies such as government departments. It may come from another part of your company, from another section or department; from branch offices; from subsidiary or associated companies, or in the form of instructions from higher management or the board. More probably the work of your section originates in some combination of these sources rather than from one only. The next thing to consider is where the output of the section goes and to what purpose.

Again it may go to any range of places in the same way as the input arrives. If it goes in the form of orders on the factory, you should try to meet the manager who receives your output and try to find out how he uses it and whether it is in the right form for him or whether it could be altered in any way which would save either your section or his work. Be cautious in your approach to this. You do not want him to think that you are trespassing on his territory or that you are trying to build your empire at his expense. Equally you should avoid entering into firm commitments to change. Rather you should undertake to study the problem and see whether the change can be made.

In parallel with this you should be studying what your section does with the input in order to prepare the various outputs. Also consider what records the section is building up and why. If the manager who held the job before you was a passenger, there will almost certainly be scope for change and improvement. Probably the section's working system was laid down years ago and has had bits built on to it to cope with changing requirements. It may well not take account of the equipment currently available in your field.

Study the work carefully till you really understand what is happening. Perhaps some of it is done by skilled technicians, craftsmen or professionals. You will not be able to do his work but you must understand what they are doing and why.

When you can see a way in which the method of working can be improved try to bring the idea out from your subordinate in discussion. If necessary just air the idea. Let them think it over and see if they come back to you with an improved proposal. Particularly try to avoid making changes suddenly, because many people are frightened of change and of new ideas.

Also it is not always easy to see all the consequences of a change at first sight. The last thing you want is a series of changes followed by changes back as the unforeseen consequences come to light. Nothing will sap the confidence of your staff quicker, except perhaps making a wrong decision and sticking to it just because you are not prepared to lose face by reversing your decision.

The Files and Their Growth

There are two particular areas of work at which you should look: the keeping of records and the submitting of reports and returns. Some records and documents have to be kept for a legal minimum period. Most or these fall in the area of the company secretary. Middle and junior line managers rarely deal with documents which have to be kept for a legal minimum of years. Correspondence dealing with contracts or staff should be kept. However, an examination of the files of the average manager will disclose that he is hoarding a mountain of paper such as internal memos and minutes of meetings held long ago and material of only passing interest. The result of hoarding past correspondence is that it requires expensive filing cabinets to house it, and the filing cabinets take up valuable space in the offices. Worst of all, because so much has been kept, it becomes difficult if not impossible to find significant correspondence when you want it. Again, take your time. After you have been in your job a few months and know what is significant in the job, start to go through the files with your secretary, chief clerk or registry clerk. This is a laborious task so the best way of tackling it is probably to put aside half an hour a day for the purpose until you have been through the lot. Take each file in turn. If the date of the last letter on the file is over a year ago and there is no continuation file consider its destruction. In going through the files, a great many letters and memos are obviously only of temporary interest such as notes giving the time and place of a meeting. These should be pulled out and destroyed. In correspondence which is two years old or more, there must be

25

something of continuing significance to make it worthwhile to retain it. When you have finished weeding the files, you should have
considerably reduced their size and number. However, if the number of files is still large, consider whether some of them can be
bundled up and stored in a cellar. When looking at documents,
consider whether you are the prime holder of the document. If you
are only holding a copy and a full file is held elsewhere in the company, it is probable that your copy can be destroyed. If the occasion
arises when you do need to refer to it, then you can borrow the
original from the full file holder. In general, managers keep too
much paper rather than too little. If a lot of paper of only short
term interest passes through your office it may be worthwhile to
mark papers not for filing but just for retention. Your secretary can
then automatically destroy them after a few days.

Reports and Returns

The question of reports and returns is a difficult one. Both the ones
you receive and the ones you submit have a self-perpetuating
momentum. Their receipt or despatch is a landmark in the calendar.
They need to be reviewed with care. Why are they prepared? For
what purpose are they used? Do they give the information which is
really needed? Is the information as well presented as it should
be? Would less information fulfil the needs and save costs in preparation? Almost certainly 50 per cent or more of the people who
receive the returns get them out of idle curiosity rather than because they will use the information. Similarly, some people reach
the stage where they regard their name on the distribution list
of an important return as a status symbol. Try to cut down the
distribution list. If photocopying costs $2\frac{1}{2}$ pence a sheet, then cutting 10 people off the distribution list of a monthly 20 page report
saves £60 a year for copying alone, let alone distribution costs and
recipient reading time. The amount may seem small to you but the
systematic pruning of unnecessary work adds up to a substantial
annual saving.

With returns coming in to you, once you have decided that you
don't need them or that less information is needed, it is fairly
straightforward to tell those from whom it comes to drop your
name from the distribution list or to chat to them about providing
you with less information.

With reports going upwards the problem is a bit greater. You
may be told that the report is essential in its present form for Mr
Big or that it is a board report. Don't be deterred, look critically

at the report yourself and draft an improved form. Depending on circumstances, the changes may be introduced gradually without saying anything. If no one comments, you have succeeded, though you may well ask yourself whether the reason for no comment is that no one reads the report anyway. However, in many circumstances you may have to approach the problem differently, particularly if you are going to alter the layout of the front page. Here you probably need to produce the old and new version for a month and put them up for consideration to the key person concerned—your own manager, Mr Big, or perhaps a particular board member. If possible present the proposal in person and explain briefly why the new version is better for the recipient: the information is clearer gives a more summarised but more up-to-date picture, draws attention to exceptions only and hence saves the recipient reading time while bringing figures needing attention more readily to his attention. If you can't present the benefits of the change in person then provide a short succinct commentary to accompany the new version.

Don't Get in a Rut

You have taken over your new managerial job and become thoroughly familiar with the job and your people. You have checked over the working methods, the files and the returns. You have made some changes and improvements. After six months you feel you have done a good job and really justified your appointment. Don't now sit back on your laurels, telling everyone what a good chap you are. This is how people get into a rut. Regularly review your activity against your job aim in the light of changing circumstances both inside the company and in the outside world. Ask yourself, how can I increase my contribution to the company's success?

four The Future Keeps Coming— Fast!

What is Your Ambition?

If you are like most managers it may be to have a quiet life with enough pay to take home to enable you to enjoy the standard of life to which you feel entitled. This might be described in other words as security with run of the mill financial rewards. Even if your ambitions are as lowly as this, pause for a moment to consider the matter. The French chose security when they choose the Maginot Line. How much real security did that buy them in 1940? In the fifties, sixties and at the time of writing in the UK a great many people are realising that security is not inherent in their jobs. The merger business is still in full flood with the inevitable reorganisations and redundancies. How many managers forty and fifty years young have found themselves hastily adjusting to the cold demands of the managerial job market? This relative insecurity is a general tendency which applies all over the modern world.

Industry and commerce throughout the Western world is concerned about costs. It is concerned to knock pennies or fractions of a penny off the cost of the components in its products. Companies may grow fat and carry passengers when markets are easy and expansion at any cost is possible. But when markets become more difficult and factories are working below capacity, the passengers are sent ashore. If they are not, then unit costs steadily rise and the competitive position of the company becomes weaker until some ruthless operator takes over. The passengers are then promptly sent ashore. In the fog and confusion of the takeover the

28

services of some effective people are dispensed with either because they are duplicating work done in the parent company or simply because their merit is not immediately recognised.

If your ambition is security with a run of the mill salary, consider carefully what price you are paying and what goods you are getting in return. Many personnel officers sell their companies to new recruits at least partly on their solidity and security of employment. Unfortunately, such dealings are not recorded—they rest on discreet face to face discussions.

Years later, perhaps not many, the victim realises he has been at the wrong end of a bargain and has bought a job which has not fulfilled the specification: *caveat emptor*. Everyone has a basic need for security, but do not be misled into thinking that we live in such a static world that you can buy security when you leave school or university. The world may change in the following forty odd years. Even the apparently most stable institution may come to grief. Security is relative. You have only to think of a hydrogen bomb on London to realise that. Even relative security is something earned by your efforts. It is not something dropped into your lap by an employer.

Time goes by and once gone is gone forever. At twenty the future stretches interminably before us and we waste our time because we do not value it. At seventy we squander it because we are conscious that the end is near and our opportunities have gone, some taken and some lost. It is sensible at any age to take stock of our position. What assets have we? How many years in full health can we hope for? How do we want to apply those assets during those years? What is our ambition? What do we really want to do with our life? Can we make a plan to achieve it?

Know Your Strengths

You may feel a bit foolish doing so, but it is well worthwhile to sit down coldly and objectively to list your strengths and to set down your ambition or aim in life. For some people this is unnecessary. They have had a clear aim since early childhood and have pursued it relentlessly. Most of us, however, are very woolly in our thinking about ourselves and where we should be going. You won't produce an answer by sitting at a table for half an hour and writing it glibly down. It will be done over several weeks or months. Just as important as writing it down will be the turning of it over in your mind. As the whole question becomes buried deeper and deeper into your mind, so the subconscious thought processes will go to work on it. As you define your aim also watch out for the constraints. It is said, and we believe that it is true, that almost anyone who wants to do so badly enough can make large sums of money, but at what price? Most people have a mix of aims. This is, on the one hand, dangerous because a mixture of aims diffuses your efforts and may lead to not achieving any of them. On the other hand, the ruthless pursuit of a single aim, be it money, position, professional excellence or recognition, may result in a very one-sided development of one's life and, when the aim is achieved, the achievement may be much less satisfying than expected.

It is a sad fact of life that the journey is often more satisfying than the destination. If you decide that your ambition in life is to become managing director of your own firm or one of comparable size you can at least look forward to a long journey. Such an ambition is to achieve something in the distant future. It provides a useful framework and a yardstick against which to measure your progress. However, you need to examine the route to achieving this ambition and establish what are the milestones on the route. These milestones provide intermediate goals which have to be achieved in order to reach the final goal. They provide the short-term stimulus of a goal, which can be seen to be achievable within a comparatively short time, say two years.

Some people might argue that it is pointless to have any longer-term aim than this. The world is changing about us. Large modern companies only have one chief executive with perhaps 50,000, perhaps 250,000 people working in the company and to set yourself the target of becoming that one man in a quarter million is so discouraging as to be a positive disincentive to effort. Why not keep your feet on the ground and set your sights simply on a management job one up from your present one? Well, for one thing, the chances of achieving a top job without a clear aim and a driving ambition to get there are pretty slight. For another, a major spur to effort is often shortage of time. If your target is to achieve the next step within two years, you are likely to concentrate your effort to a much greater extent than if you see twenty years ahead of you to make the step.

One's long-term aim should, of course, be realistic, but that does not mean too modest. Experience suggests that the really vital ingredient in success is neither ability nor intelligence. It is determination. An accepted principle of war is to reinforce success. This can be applied in the war we wage to build our future. We identify our strengths and plan to build on them. We identify our weaknesses and plan to protect ourselves from them.

30

Know Your Weaknesses

The whole question of weaknesses in humans as in companies is a fascinating one. The attitude of many, if not most, people is to devote a disproportionate time to their weaknesses. They worry about them. Take a simple example. Suppose one spells words wrongly and has no feeling for correct spelling. One man will keep a dictionary on his desk and look up every word of more than one syllable as he goes along. His output of written work will fall drastically. Sometimes he will be forced to speed up and ridiculous mistakes will appear in the end product, an important report or customer letter, with unfortunate results. Another man will take a different approach. He will recognise his weakness and protect himself by employing a secretary who is strong on spelling. He will make it clear to her that he can't spell and relies on her to correct the spelling in anything he drafts by hand.

This may seem an over-simple example but the same principle applies in more complex situations. A manager, who is good with people but bad at figures, makes sure he either has a colleague who is good with figures or someone on his staff, thus covering his weakness. Everyone has some weakness; those who are successful recognise the fact and protect themselves, while concentrating their effort on the area in which they are strong.

The External Environment

Having defined your objective and identified your strengths and weaknesses, you have to go on to consider what other factors affect the plan. Major factors are the conditions inside your present company, its future prospects and the condition of the industry (or branch of commerce) generally. As part of your job you should, as a go-ahead manager, study these factors and know something of them. In the more limited context of your own future it is desirable to form some opinion about the structure of management in your own company. Has the company developed a management development programme? If so, you may be able to deduce your prospects in the company. Is there anything to be learnt from the age structure of the existing management? Is there a high proportion of managers due for retirement in the next five years or are most of the management jobs above you filled by people in their forties?

Is there evidence of any bias in filling senior jobs? Is there any specially favoured class of people who fill the top jobs? This might be most easily identified in those family firms where senior

31

jobs are normally filled by family members. There may be a bias towards graduates or graduates from a particular university or even college. After a merger, promotions by some coincidence may always come from one 'side' of the firm and the demotions mainly from the other. If you are on the wrong side, it is something to watch. The outstanding man can generally make his way in the face of difficulties such as these. However, it may be a pointer towards moving to another company to secure a better future. In making an assessment of these factors, make them on your own judgement and try equally to avoid being over-influenced by the hard luck stories of those who failed to make it and the propaganda of the personnel manager.

One decision which has to be made fairly early in your career is whether you intend to make a career for life with one company or whether you deliberately intend to make one or more moves to broaden your experience. Circumstances may of course force a change of decision later. There are plenty of examples of both methods leading to successful careers. People without formal qualifications probably find it easier to make progress by staying with one company. They build up their reputation and their lack of paper qualifications is overlooked or forgotten.

A factor to be considered is the rate and direction of change in your company and industry. Inevitably the fast expanding modern industries like computers act as a magnet for the bright and ambitious young. So long as the rate of expansion is kept up prospects are good and the competition helps to keep you on your toes. Similarly a contracting industry finds it difficult to attract new entrants and may be heavily over-weighted with elderly managers. There may be, despite the apparently generally gloomy prospects, a very good chance for the determined young manager.

Is the contraction taking place because of a drop in the demand or because markets are being lost? Is it due to failure to develop new products? Is it due to fashion? Is it due to overseas competition, national tariffs or policies? Is expansion due to a temporary lead in technology, to protection or some other artificial cause? Is the industry dominated by a single company or small group of companies? Are there hundreds of small independent companies? Is there a trend towards consolidation by merger or takeover? Is there anything about the industry which favours large-scale or small-scale operation? Is it the sort of industry where new small firms can enter with comparative ease?

Your Plans for Your Future

All these factors and many more have a bearing on your plan for the future. It is worth giving conscious thought to each of them. Having considered all the factors, the next step is to identify all the possible ways in which you could achieve your final objective. Each of these possibilities will have both advantages and disadvantages, which should be weighed up. Finally the most practicable or most attractive is chosen and worked out in some detail.

The detail of the plan is what you need to do to achieve your objective. Even if you have decided to achieve your aim of becoming managing director by marrying the boss's daughter, some planning effort is required. It may also be desirable to make some other preparation to enable you to perform the duties when the mantle falls on you.

Money Matters

One factor that sooner or later affects most people's future is money. Many managers plan their personal financial affairs so badly that they cannot afford to risk losing their jobs; they can only afford to change jobs if they go straight from the old job to the new with all expenses paid. The prospect of redundancy becomes a permanent underlying worry, sapping their confidence. Studies in the UK have suggested that the majority of managers go through life with very little saving. The bulk of their saving tends to be in the form of their house, acquired on mortgage, and in the form of contributions to their company's pension fund. The result is to limit the manager's independence of outlook and to tie him firmly to his existing company even when its prospects are declining.

Independence is not, of course, solely a matter of money. However, the average man feels happier when he has enough financial backing to know that losing his job will not have an immediate impact on his family. We believe that one essential step for every manager planning his future is to plan his own financial affairs in such a way as to provide himself with a capital sum. The management of his own capital is an education in itself; it accustoms him to examining results, which matter to him, to see whether they were satisfactory and if not where he went wrong. More important, it can provide the independence and backing necessary if he decides he wants to change not just his job but his whole career. If he finds himself in a boring rut he can break out of it.

D

If he really wants to back his own ideas and set up his own business, the possession of some capital makes this possible.

Building up capital requires three things. First earning the necessary money, second saving a proportion of earnings and thirdly investing it to the best advantage. Saving like so many other things is a matter of setting realistic objectives and having the determination to achieve them. There is merit in Micawber's guide to happiness. Living within one's income provides a margin, which not only leads to ease of mind but also provides the wherewithal to start accumulating some capital. The sums you can save initially may be quite small but it has been convincingly demonstrated that a man saving £100 a year throughout his working life can without undue risk accumulate £100,000 by the time he retires. By saving more or taking some risks, greater sums can be achieved earlier. Jim Slater starting with a sum of £2,000 in 1962 had built his personal fortune up to over £4,000,000 by the end of 1970. This is of course outstanding and most unusual, but our point is that there is no reason why any manager should not build up an appreciable capital sum. If income is always spent up to the hilt, there is a case for ignoring the advent of the next pay rise so far as spending is concerned; just save it! How the money, once saved, should be invested is too large a subject for us to cover here. Reading a good elementary book such as the *Investors Chronicle Beginners Please* is a good start. This can be supplemented by reading the *Financial Times* and *The Investors' Chronicle*.

In summary, the effective manager knows what he wants to do with his life, clearly identifies his own objectives and makes a plan to achieve them. In doing so he arms himself with as much flexibility as possible both by looking to his own training and development and also by accumulating enough capital to give him some independence.

five Keeping Tabs

Your Office

In a great measure your success as a manager will depend on the way in which you organise your own office and papers. The successful manager has considerable command of detail, while managers who flop generally cannot be bothered with it. A well organised office, with the information you really need readily available, makes the difference between the really effective manager and the well meaning bumbler. It can also reduce the strain on you and reduce the hazards to your health.

Companies vary in their attitude to providing and furnishing offices for their managers. Some provide for managers according to a scale: a manager is provided with so many square feet of space, a desk and chair of a given size and style and so many visitors' chairs according to his seniority and status. In others, the new manager is given his predecessor's office or whatever room is available and left to get on with it.

In the first few days in your new job take stock of your new office. You probably can't do much about the size or shape. For a junior manager about 100 square feet of space is likely to be provided. If you are lucky you may get more, if unlucky less. Make sure it is clean, well lit and properly ventilated. It may seem odd to mention these points but it is surprising how many junior managers' offices are plain dirty. This is particularly the case in offices in factory blocks and where large residential houses have been converted for use as offices. The floor may not be carpeted but there is no excuse for it being covered with dust and odd pieces of paper and cigarette ends. Find out who is responsible for cleaning and politely but firmly insist that your office is cleaned. If there is no carpet on the floor try to get it polished, scrubbed or stained as appropriate. Arrange for the floor to be swept/Hoovered every day thereafter. Windows make a great deal of difference to an office. Needless to say they should be cleaned both inside and out to allow the maximum light into the office. If they face south and catch the direct sun in the summer consider the possibility of having venetian blinds or curtains fitted. Curtains tend to be a bit of a dust trap. Unless they are kept clean and tidy they make your office look scruffy.

The greatest contribution to comfort at work is having adequate light to work in. Try to place your desk where you get the maximum natural light. Next make sure that when natural light is insufficient, in the evening and early morning for instance, that you have adequate artificial light. A single 60 watt bulb dangled from the centre of the ceiling is not good enough. If the main light fitting is too remote from your desk and does not provide a strong enough light source, supplement it by having a reading lamp on your desk. If you have too much trouble with your administrator, ask him if the office meets the requirements of the Offices, Shops and Railway Premises Act.

Your Desk

Most managers spend a high proportion of their day behind their desk. It, together with the chair in which he sits, is probably the second most important piece of furniture in his life. It must be level as even the most indolent manager will find it inconvenient if all four desk legs do not meet the floor at the same time. The desk will, in these circumstances, rock and slop the tea into his saucer. More energetic managers will find it a continual irritation and distraction, so get it fixed right away. As well as providing a smooth working surface, your desk provides some useful personal storage space. The better modern desks for managers usually include a couple of large drawers and two small drawers. One of the large ones is usually fitted out to carry suspended files. This should be lockable and can be used to house your confidential files and those to which you constantly need to refer.

We are firm believers in the clear desk top policy. Each day when you leave work, your desk top should be left completely clear. If it is not, the office cleaner has the perfect excuse for never polishing your desk. If your desk top is littered with papers the chances are that some vital piece of paper will fall onto the floor and be swept away with the rubbish. There is also the general question of security. Among the desk-top papers may be information about new products, marketing strategy, pricing policy, research and development information or staff movements, salaries and expenses. In the wrong hands any of these documents could be used to the detriment of the company. Where someone may feel justified in looking at papers on your desk top, or lift them 'by mistake', they are unlikely to go through your drawers, even the unlocked ones, unless they are deliberately set on industrial espionage. Lastly the mere fact of packing away the loose papers each evening and un-packing them the following morning is likely to prompt you to sort them out and deal with them. The senior manager will prob-ably have this side of things dealt with by his executive secretary. For the more junior manager, the answer is probably to put aside the second large drawer of his desk entirely for this purpose. Last thing at night, he opens it and drops in his in-tray plus any loose papers on which he is working. The out-tray should have been cleared just before the end of the day; but if he works later and there are papers in it, then it too should be dropped into the drawer.

Even if you do not smoke, have an ashtray in your office for those of your visitors who do. If you deal with people from out-side the firm, it is probably a good idea to have some matches in the drawer of your desk and possibly cigarettes as well. Try to have at least two comfortable chairs for visitors. By comfortable we do not mean plush, just reasonably comfortable upright chairs, preferably with a padded seat.

Your Secretary

As a junior manager you will probably be allowed the services of a secretary or at least share one with another junior manager. A secretary is not just a status symbol nor is she just a decorative feature of the outer office. Properly selected and used a good secretary will greatly add to your effectiveness. A poor secretary can reduce your effectiveness and lead you into difficulties with your own manager, your staff and colleagues, not to mention custo-mers and suppliers.

The first thing to get clear in your mind is why have a secretary at all? In this day there are dictaphones and typing pools, which can handle your dictation and typing as effectively and sometimes more so than a secretary. The canteen or tea lady can probably be persuaded to bring tea and coffee to your office. The receptionist will look after your visitors and usher them around to your office. So why have a secretary? A secretary has a more important role to play. Apart from helping you to do your work, she should literally increase your capacity for work by a third to a half. She will only do this if you are clear about how this can be done.

Your secretary should be an extension of yourself. Encourage her to do as much of your work as she is able to do. Apart from the obvious advantage that it reduces your work load and increases your effectiveness, it is also good for her. It gives added interest to her working day and prevents her getting bored. Instead of dictating routine replies to letters or memorandum, just tell her to reply 'yes' or 'thank him' or 'next Monday at 3.00 p.m.' This can be scribbled on the letter or you can go through a pile with her just making a brief comment on each. She can then go away and compose suitable replies at her typewriter. As you get used to working together, it should be possible to hand over most of your routine or near routine correspondence to her. When you are away from the office for a few days or on holiday, it should be possible for her to sort through your correspondence as it comes in. Letters, which she cannot herself deal with, she will pass on to one of your staff, who can prepare a reply. Letters she can deal with, she will either reply to on your behalf or have a reply typed and ready for your signature on your first day back in the office.

Much of the routine of your office can be handled by your secretary. She will of course make travel arrangements for you, booking hotels, obtaining tickets and seat reservations, arranging cars and providing maps and itineraries. She should keep a holiday and sickness record for all the people who report directly to you.

A good secretary will also act as a guard and keep away unwelcome visitors and telephone calls. As we have seen in discussing your time, it is necessary to set aside some quite large chunks of time during the working day to enable you to tackle the jobs which need care and thought. Your secretary can make sure that you are not disturbed during these periods. She must, however, use her discretion. She must have enough sense not to tell the managing director that you never speak to anyone before ten in the morning, if he should happen to come through on the phone. In letting your secretary act as a dragon to keep away unwanted visitors you must be careful that she does not keep away people you ought to see. Some grown men are very shy. Such a man may have something of critical importance to say to you but having been turned away by the dragon, it may be days before he summons up courage to try again. It may be a delay which costs your company thousands of pounds. So try to check up unobtrusively on the way she handles your visitors.

If you handle small sums of petty cash, your secretary can probably take care of this for you and keep the necessary accounts. She can keep an account of your expenses and see that they are claimed and paid. If you are provided with Luncheon Vouchers in bulk for your staff, she can keep the necessary records and issue them.

Most secretaries in British industrial and commercial concerns are under-worked. Don't be afraid of over-working yours; it's surprising how much work an efficient secretary can get through in a day.

Keeping Abreast

As well as keeping tabs on his own immediate job, any manager should make sure that he knows as much as possible about his company and the business or industry in which it operates. He should also make sure that he keeps himself broadly abreast of current affairs.

To keep abreast of current affairs the manager should read at least one national newspaper each day. The papers which carry most business news are probably *The Financial Times* and *The Times*. Two other serious papers, *The Guardian* and *Daily Telegraph*, also contain an appreciable amount of business news. In reading at least one of these papers, read also the main items of home and overseas news and the leading articles, which generally cover the important topics of the day. Time spent in reading the *Economist* each week will not be wasted. It gives wide coverage to news and views on matters of importance to national and international business. As well as this general background and reading, the young manager should also read the trade press of his own industry and the journals serving his own speciality. For instance a data processing manager in a firm operating in the textile industry, will read computer journals such as *Data Systems* and *Dataweek* as well as the journals covering the textile industry.

There is something to be said for keeping a cuttings file or book. Items of interest in the press can be marked by you for cutting out by your secretary. Each cutting should be marked with the name of the publication from which it has been cut and the date or issue number. Cuttings giving factual information and opinions about your own company, about industry prospects and your main competitors and customers are useful.

Some companies are prepared to provide their managers with

copies of *The Financial Times* or *The Times*. If yours does not, it may be worth trying to persuade your manager that the cost represents a reasonable expense. Be careful, however, as there is at least one leader of industry who believes that his managers should buy their own papers and read them in their own time. Whether your company encourages it or not, it is in your own interests to keep up to date. If you commute to work by train it is no hardship to spend the time in useful reading.

Most large companies have a central library which not only holds a stock of books but also subscribes to the leading journals in the fields in which it operates. These are usually circulated to managers on demand. Because so many people wish to read such journals, they frequently do not reach junior managers until they have become history. If you cannot make up the deficiency by charging the subscription of the leading journal of interest in your field to your section budget, you should consider buying at least one leading journal from your own pocket.

There is of course one kind of journal or newspaper available to you without charge. This is the controlled circulation paper. These papers are paid for by advertisers and circulated without charge to people who are believed likely to be interested in the advertisements. For instance, any manager concerned with data processing can apply to be put on the free circulation list of *Dataweek*. Although free, magazines of this sort contain editorial matter of interest. As well as information about new products, appointments and promotions in the industry, there are articles on subjects of interest and editorial comment on current problems. Controlled circulation magazines provide particularly good cover in the computer and office services field. There are also magazines aimed specifically at managers, though generally they try to build up their list from senior rather than junior managers. Examples are *International Management* and *Business Administration*.

The journals and other publications of professional associations, such as the British Institute of Management and the Institute of Marketing, are a rich source of relevant background information for managers. They help to keep him in touch with management practice.

Know Your Own Company

In small companies, the junior manager may be kept fairly fully in the picture about the activities of his own company without much effort on his part. In a large company it is probably a very different matter. Like the rest of the staff he will probably receive copies of the company house magazine or news sheet and some comments or instructions from his own manager. This is not enough. The main published source of information about a public company is the annual report and accounts. You should obtain and study these each year as well as reading the newspaper comment on them. In some companies it is possible to obtain a copy of the report and accounts by asking the secretary's department. If this proves difficult, the manager of your bank branch can probably obtain a copy for you. To be sure of getting both annual and interim accounts, there is a lot to be said for buying a few shares in the company in which you work. This can be done quite simply through your bank manager. In most companies you can buy as few as ten shares, or even one. This entitles you to attend, speak and vote at the annual general meeting as well as receiving the reports.

Once obtained the annual report should be studied carefully, including particularly the figures and footnotes. We cover in greater detail in a later chapter the subject of balance sheets and profit and loss accounts. The sort of figures which it is useful for you to know about your company are:

1 Its size in terms of:
    Number of employees.
    Capital employed.
    Annual turnover.
    Annual profit before and after tax.
2 Management ratios:
    Turnover per employee.
    Profit per employee.
    Return on assets employed.
    Return on turnover.

Over a period it is desirable to know the trend in these figures. For instance, is the turnover per employee steadily increasing year by year, is it static, erratic or steadily declining?

Apart from the figures build up a picture of the company. What products does it have? Who buys them—other companies, the retail trade or who? Does it sell branded goods and if so under what brands? Where are its main establishments at home and abroad? What subsidiary and associated companies does it have? Does any company or individual have a major shareholding in it?

Most large companies compete with a fairly limited number of companies at home and abroad. If possible a picture of their activities should be built up as well. In particular it is interesting to compare the basic statistics and trends of your main competitors with those of your own company. This will of course be done in a professional way somewhere in the corporate headquarters of the company. However, it is likely to make you a better informed manager, better able to accept promotion within the company if you have carried out your own study. You may be able to spend some working time on this but you may have to devote your own time to it. If you are ambitious, it is time well spent.

six Decision Making

Your first decision: delegate! Wherever and whenever you can, delegate such decision making as is within the capabilities of your staff, to your staff. Save yourself for the big ones. Guide your staff by all means, encourage them to think their decisions through thoroughly before they act. Educate them in the decision making processes which underpin all decisions but let them make decisions and the mistakes that will be inevitable to enable them to grow.

Decision making follows a logical pattern whether the decision at the end looks logical to those who have to implement it or are affected by it.

Initial Reactions

UNDERSTANDING

Firstly a decision demands a need for a decision; a problem or a question must be posed. That seems a bit obvious but do we understand what that problem or question really is? Most of us in fact find it far easier to answer questions that were never asked. Our favourite example of this is the committee. A committee meets nominally to discuss what appears to be a simple issue. Without even trying the meeting drifts off into philosophical questions that probably have no answer, but on such occasions we're all such jolly good philosophers and poor decision makers that we find philosophy far easier. *First reveal the question that is being asked: stark, clear, naked, denuded of all frills.*

43

WILL THE REAL QUESTION PLEASE STAND UP

Secondly, after we've revealed the question, ask ourselves is the question the one that ought to be asked?

In a manufacturing company we know there was much ado about making some power supplies from basic parts rather than buying them in as completed units.

The engineers were arguing the case that their design was much better and certainly the technical performance and reliability of the bought-out units left much to be desired. The manufacturing of the units it was thought could be subcontracted as the factory was busy. The question put to the engineering and manufacturing director was 'Shall we do it?' backed by various information on the desirability of the exercise. The director, taking the correct steps said firstly 'Do I understand the question and the reasons behind the question?' Yes, he felt he did. The marketing director agreed with the diagnosis of the danger in continuing to buy the complete units and was confident the 'in house' design would be better as far as he understood the matter.

The director whose decision it was then asked himself the second question in the decision making process. It all sounds right, but is it the right question? He then asked for more information on the factory loading, whether any work in hand could be subcontracted to make room for the power supply. The information was very revealing. It was in fact comparatively easy to offload work on some simple electronic assemblies to a competent subcontractor, while retaining the more complex power supply unit under their direct care. The director now decided to answer the real question that should perhaps have been revealed in the first place. 'Yes we will make the power supplies, but in our own factory, not by a subcontractor. In this way we control more directly a critical item.'

RESPONSIBILITY

At this stage it should also be clear not only what is the real question but whether we should make the decision, hand it down to one of our staff if we have not done so already or pass the problem higher within our company. It is as bad to make decisions without having the competence or organisational status to do so as it is to abrogate our proper responsibility. The decision to be made may have far reaching effects in the company the importance of which we are not in a position to judge. The decision may create precedents of deep significance in the company. Depending on your power and scope within your company will be your decision to pass the problem higher.

CURRENT THINKING

Fourthly, in our steps to decision making we should always associate the question or problem with what is normal to our line of business or to current trends. Are we trying to pose a problem out of context with company or people abilities? Is the question an impossible one? Not just the honest wrong question as in our previous step, but having an unreality, a falseness, being apart from current thinking. We have to ask these things to create that awareness of the need for extra care when such evidence exists.

These are the immediate reactions to the problem posed. We must now start the preliminary actions which must precede a decision.

Preliminary Actions

TIMING

One of the first actions should be to determine when the decision must be made. This dictates how long you can wait before making a decision. It may be too early for the decision, in which case you may take more time on the problem if it appears to warrant it. As you look at the problem it may become obvious that it is already too late to make any useful decision at all. Is this the right time is a question we must ask. Unnecessarily hurried decisions can be just as dangerous as decisions that are too late. However, if your diagnosis is that the decision is urgent then take the decision if in your province to do so after you have carried out the minimum necessary checks. Remember Montrose's famous lines:

> 'He either fears his fate too much,
> Or his deserts are small,
> Who durst not put it to the touch
> To win or lose it all.'

We hope that all our decisions don't involve winning or losing it all whatever 'it' means! In this connection one of the important preliminary actions must be the risk assessment.

ASSESSMENT OF RISK

In every decision there is an element of risk. All decisions involve some judgement and the future is yet an uncharted mystery. Judgement and future equals risk. We must try to gauge that risk in money or people terms against the reward that may also stem from the decision. Whether we can ever have a neat balance sheet in quantified terms is debatable, but we should at least be able to write down the pros and cons and make our judgements on that basis.

Sometimes, of course, we have a choice based on financial comparisons. We say more about this in Chapter 16. Take the case of the chairman of one of our large furniture makers who confided to us one of his problems in the timing of decisions and assessment of risks. All the estimates and predictions he could get from his experts together with current selling figures indicated some downturn in the volume of trade. It looked as though the decision he may have to make would be to shut down one of his smaller factories and make staff redundant. Was this the right time for this decision? Because the savings from such a move would take time to come into effect it was no good waiting until the trade had declined to a point where his profits were declining faster than they should be. If the trade was really going to decline, due, perhaps, to various Government measures and other reasons, he must act. The chairman decided to look at the question again from the viewpoint of a completely alternative course.

ALTERNATIVES

Was there an alternative course whereby the slackening of the furniture trade and the keeping open of the factory could be reconciled? The company was, fortunately, not short of liquid assets and a possible alternative course was found after a rapid but hard search. Nearby was another company making special furniture for export and who needed both extra capacity and finance. The chairman came to an amicable agreement with them, bought in shares and provided more finance. Factory capacity was able to be added to the export business as the home furniture trade declined below full capacity level. There were also side advantages in getting a foot into the export business. We should always look for alternatives in our decision making as there may be an absolutely different way of solving a problem to that first envisaged. In searching for alternatives we must try to keep as open a mind as we can to the possibilities that may exist. Unfortunately some questions seem to demand just one answer and herein lies a danger for the manager. He is not really making a decision at all, just saying yes. Decision making must mean searching for alternatives.

CRITICAL FACTORS AND FACT FINDING

If you can find the key factor early in your search for facts you may save a lot of time and money. Suppose you have to make a decision whether to proceed to the experimental stage with a new domestic tape recorder. It is going to play longer and with more fidelity than any model on the market. It also has to be very small in size. You get all the facts from your company, there are no technological problems, no manufacturing problems and it looks all set.

You look at the project to see what is the item least under your control: the magnetic tape. You have it checked again and find that it would have to be specially made at an exorbitant cost. You stop the project; you make a decision that will save your company money. If you think it was so obvious that nobody would actually get as far as that example did, you would be wrong and some companies have gone right up the wrong road with their pet projects and lost a lot of money. It happens almost daily because the questions that are essential to good decisions are not asked early enough.

Take another, totally different case that we know about. A small village shop changed ownership and the new owner found that by good marketing in the shop he raised his turnover by 40 per cent. He added new lines to grocery, stationery and allied lines. The business continued to develop. There was no hardware shop in the village so he spent several hundred pounds on additional space next to his existing shop and packed it with hardware, paints and other similar goods. The turnover from this side of the business was abysmal. He wondered where he had gone wrong. Everything else sold all right so why not the paints, etc? The answer, when he really analysed the problem, was not difficult. The women of the village liked to shop there for groceries and other basic items; buses were difficult to the town and he was fairly competitive in his prices in any case. When it came to hardware and paints, however, the men went to the town where a very large hardware and builders merchants was situated. The village store could not compete as a side line business. In fact, what the shop owner did was to sell off the paints and hardware cheaply and expand the provisions section. He never looked back after that, but he lost about a hundred pounds on the paints through missing the key factor. It is interesting to reflect, however, in this story whether he would have expanded his provisions anyway. He is not sure and says that only when the room was available did he make that decision. In this case it may have been all to the good, but the moral is clear.

Making the Decision

The steps to the decision have been these:

> Understanding the problem.
> Making sure you have the right question.
> Assessing whether it is your responsibility to make the decision.
> Checking whether the question is feasible.
> Looking at the timing needed for the decision.
> Assessing the risks.
> Seeing what alternatives exist.
> Searching for critical factors.

You are now ready to make the decision and how you make it is important. The content of what you say must accurately reflect what you want to say. Too often have good decisions been marred by poor explanations. The people who receive the decision must know what to do without doubt, even more so if the decision is an urgent one. We say more about clarity and non-ambiguity in the chapter on communications.

It is important when you make the decision to know who you must tell; there may be a series of people who, unless you tell all of them, cannot properly implement your decision. You must have planned in advance how to deal with any effects from your decision. It may be necessary in some cases to accompany your decision with explanations and answers to probable questions that may arise. What we are doing is to make sure that our decision is clear and final. A story told to us by a builder friend of ours illustrates what can happen if decisions are not made properly. The chief contracts manager issued an instruction to his contract managers on various sites.

> 'To improve our costing accuracy per site and to give you (the site manager) more information about the site profit you will personally check all invoices before we pass them for payment.'

In essence this was a sensible request, but unfortunately the decision had not been thought about deeply enough and the questions soon started to roll in:

'Have I got to come down to the office, it's about a hundred miles you know?'
'Are you going to post them?'
'How do I know when you've got invoices?'
'What about the advice notes, will they do?'

In fact, nobody really knew how to deal with what seemed a simple enough decision and request. The next decision was that 'We will post them to the sites.' This started off and the first realisation of trouble was when a supplier cut off supplies at one site because the account, due weekly, had not been paid. An examination showed that invoices were now being held in transit and checking, etc, for well over a week. A further decision was made, 'We will send a copy invoice to the sites.' Unfortunately this could not prevent some invoices having to be paid at Head Office without knowing whether they were correct as to deliveries to the site.

As can be seen the situation was in a muddle. It was a good idea in the first place, but was not thought out properly before the decision was made. What happened in fact was that copies went out for a while and the scheme was then dropped. The company went back to their previous system. About six months later another attempt was made to tighten up the system: this time it was thought out more thoroughly; simple changes were made to the sites' paperwork system and delivery returns sent in with other papers that had to come in regularly.

Checking the Action

The last thing that must be done is to check the action to see if the decision has been received correctly and work done. There are always cases where receivers of information stemming from decisions don't get it right and put into action work that is not quite that required. Arising from the usual communication weaknesses that are so prevalent it is important to check the action, especially if more than one level of command is involved. This is not always as easy as it sounds. Managers cannot walk around regularly and check with staff two or three levels below and say 'Did your manager pass on my decision correctly!' If the decision is important and significant to several management levels, particularly in the context in which it is stated, then it may be better to circulate it in written form.

E

49

"HE'S NOT SO BAD — HE'S GOT A PH.D IN MANAGEMENT SCIENCE"

part two Managing People

seven Setting People Free to Perform

Management is People

Management is people. Being a manager is different. It is different because you do your work through the minds and hands of other people. The art of the manager lies in getting other people to work effectively to achieve objectives.

Some people have been managing others since the dawn of history. There have always been those who believed in the Brute Force and Bloody Ignorance approach. The 'managers' of Phoenician galleys chained slaves to the oars and employed foremen with whips to stand over them to make sure they pulled together. In its time this was a sound enough system of management. The social climate of the time permitted it and for the slaves there was no acceptable alternative available.

Slavery disappeared gradually throughout the world, but the BF and BI managers still had powerful sanctions to hand. Chief of these was the right to sack without question and at the same time to blacken a man or woman's reputation; in other words to keep employees in fear that they and their families would starve if they did not toe the line. At one time a whole range of fines and other punishments were also available to the manager.

There have always been a few managers who have taken a more enlightened view. This number has increased rapidly in the sixties and seventies, spurred on by a social climate which is no longer conducive to the success of BF and BI methods.

The Modern Management Setting

Most advanced industrial countries try to operate their economies at such a level that the majority of the working population are in employment. What unemployment there is now, is confined in the main to those who for one reason or another are unemployable or those who are unemployed for a short period on changing their jobs. There are few industrial countries where a man's family will starve if he is out of work. So far from employers being able to use the sack as a sanction, most managers are far more concerned about how to retain existing staff and how to fill vacancies with competent and effective staff.

As well as the change in the social climate there has been a major change in the nature of work. This was very gradual in the twenties and forties but by the sixties and seventies change was very rapid.

A hundred years ago only a very few people worked with their minds. The majority were labourers with a few skilled craftsmen who learned their craft in their teens and practised it through the rest of their lives. The number of office workers was a tiny fraction of the number who fill the offices of modern commercial and industrial enterprises. Today the situation has changed and is still rapidly changing. Automation and the introduction of computers have reduced the number of routine non-thinking jobs. The increasing pace of change has resulted in people being more willing to change not just their jobs, but also their trade or profession as they seek out the opportunities to improve their lot. Many people look forward quite happily to the idea of working in two or three entirely unrelated fields in the course of their working lifetime.

All this has a considerable impact on how successful managers manage people. People no longer work without thought. They are no longer willing to do something merely because they are told to do so. A good manager does not expect them to do so.

In this modern world, you, the manager, must create a climate in which your people bring their minds to work with them and really apply themselves to their jobs.

People do Know Their Jobs

It is quite common when doing systems studies prior to the introduction of a computer system to find that a manager will give you a description of how his system works. The experienced systems man then spends some time with the people who do the work. In most cases the real system is very different from the one described by the manager. Not only different, but better. It is better because it has come to terms with realities. It deals with the exceptions and inconsistencies. It cuts the corners and sorts out the real priorities. We should not be too surprised that the man who is closest to a job, the man who is actually doing it, has the best knowledge of how it is done. This is as true of a factory job as it is of an office job. The man who knows the job and is interested in it quickly appreciates the effects which change will have on the job. He will know how the job can be improved and done more efficiently to the firm's advantage. He will also know whether the changes are likely to benefit him by making his day's work easier, more interesting or more profitable. How far this knowledge will be applied to the firm's benefit will depend to a great extent on the man's attitude to the firm and his relationship with his manager.

Some managers are extraordinarily successful simply because they listen to what their people have to say and then make use of their ideas. There are those who explain the success of consultant firms by saying that they go into a firm, listen to everyone and then make a report serving up the best ideas that have come from the people they have spoken to, all at a fee of about £50 a day. It is much cheaper and more effective for managers to listen to their own staff.

So how do we set about the problem of enlisting the interests and energies of people for the benefit of their jobs and the organisation for which they work? The first point is to remember that people are human; they are not machines. They are likely to have their fair share of human failings as well as virtues. On the whole people respond to trust being placed in them. Lack of trust often poses a challenge to people. For instance, in an organisation which has a very strict control over timekeeping there is likely to exist an unspoken challenge to outwit the system and arrive half an hour late each day without the system detecting the fact. Similarly most restrictive rules will provoke opposition and will lead to an enormous waste of time as people try to circumvent the system. Rules must be kept to a minimum and people's energies harnessed postively to produce effective work.

Specifying the Job

It may seem obvious to say that the first necessity is that people should know what they are required to do and why. A man who does not know what to do cannot perform at all. In all but the manual or routine jobs a man who does not know 'why' will not perform effectively. To give of their best performance the people who work for you, your people, must have a clear idea of what you expect from them. It is not sufficient that they have a list of tasks to be performed. This may be sufficient for someone who is being used as a mere replacement for horsepower. It is not good enough where you expect people to devote their minds and intelligence, their imagination and creative abilities to the furtherance of your objectives. Such cases are the cases which occur in modern industry and commerce. For these people, the modern knowledge workers, you must make your aims clear and enlist their sympathy and determination to achieve those aims.

In preparing your people for their jobs, the first thing therefore is to make sure that they understand what you are setting out to achieve. Next they must have clearly their own purpose, the part which they must play in achieving the aim. It is highly desirable that you spell out the major tasks which you require them to perform as part of that purpose. Finally they must know to whom they are responsible, whether to you or someone else.

In a tight knit group working closely together it may be possible for this all to be done by word of mouth, particularly in a rapidly changing situation. In most normal circumstances it is usual to put this job description in writing. Great care must be taken over the wording of the 'purpose'. The whole job description should be discussed with the person concerned to make quite sure that he understands the same things from it that you do. In fact, after an initial discussion of the job it is quite a good idea to make each of your people write the first draft of his own job description. It can then be refined in discussion with him. In this way it should be possible to obtain his complete understanding of what is required and a commitment to doing it.

Apart from the job description it must be clear to each person when you want to hear from him and what. Ideally you will want him to report his progress on some basis, probably routine confirmation that all is going well according to plan with exceptions stated and a statement of how they will be put right. Reports may be a set of figures, quantifying his performance. In this case they must be figures which really are meaningful to you and which will throw up evidence of things going wrong long before they reach the desperate stage. The object of such reporting is to enable you to control the work for which you are responsible. The report should come naturally out of the needs of the work of your subordinates and should not be a great additional load superimposed on his normal work load and irrelevant to it.

The whole aim of your job descriptions and your reporting system is to harness the abilities of your people to the job in hand and to give them as free a hand as possible to make the greatest contribution of which they are capable. You must not be restrictive in the job description. The object is not to stifle the drive and imagination of your people, but rather to encourage them to seek out, recognise and exploit their opportunities for the benefit of the organisation.

People are Human

Getting a man's job clearly specified and understood is only the first step towards harnessing the whole man and all his energy to the job. The good effects of a clearly understood job specification can very quickly be destroyed if your subsequent actions appear to contradict the trust and spirit of partnership implied in the specification. Your attitude to the man must be consistent.

There is an old adage that you should 'do unto others as you would be done by'. In other words, don't complain that your boss is always interfering and won't leave you in peace to get on with the job, and then go and do the selfsame thing with your own staff.

The people who work for you are human beings the same as you are. Some of their interests will not be the same as yours, but their basic humanity is the same. They have the same human aspirations and fears as you do. Treat the people who work for you with normal politeness and courtesy. If you really feel you must be overbearing and rude, try it out on your boss instead since he won't have to put up with it. If you behave like a pig with your staff, their resentment will be real even if it is hidden. People who feel resentful do not give of their best.

Most people are fearful of the unknown, hence the considerable opposition to change. The mere suspicion that change is coming, for instance after a takeover, may cause fear and a consequent reduction in efficiency. A basic rule for all managers is, therefore, 'Always keep your people in the picture.' People should always be consulted about changes from the very earliest stages. This is important for two reasons. First they may contribute ideas which will lead to the change being more effective. Second the consultation before a firm plan has been established is an act of consideration, which lets people feel that they can influence the plan. It is not being dictated to them. They can see it evolve, make their contribution and hopefully see it as a logical outcome of the situation which exists.

Loyalty is Two Way

We shall in the next chapter consider how people's performance should be measured and how they can be encouraged to improve. There is, however, one other essential factor in setting people free to perform. They must believe that you will look after their interest. It is of the utmost importance that you deal fairly and honestly with your people, and that they should see that this is the case. On no account must you knuckle under to a 'personnel ruling' or a higher management decision which is unjust in its impact on your people. Loyalty is a two-way matter. You cannot expect loyalty from your people if you are not loyal to them. You must be prepared to fight for your staff.

eight Reward and Promotion

Introduction

We have talked about setting people free to perform. If they do perform well they should be rewarded for their performance. If a good performance is to be kept up, people should know that their performance is being assessed in some systematic fashion and that when that assessment justifies it, they will be suitably rewarded.

Performance Review

The tools used for this assessment are the performance review and the appraisal interview. The aims of the review form and the associated appraisal interview are:

1 To look systematically at how a man has performed in relation to the objectives set him for the period under review (generally a year).
2 To show the man how his manager views his performance.
3 To let the man give his own views on his performance and on his career ambitions.
4 To record the manager's opinion of how the man should be employed in the future.
5 To identify the man's needs for training and development in relation to his performance, his ambitions and his future planned employment.

The completed review also provides a basis on which to decide on what reward the man should be given for the period under review.

The Review Form

This should give the normal administrative details: name, job, age, place of employment, length of time in present job and in company. This should be followed by a restatement of the job purpose, taken from the man's job description.

The meat of the form comes in a statement of the tasks which the man had to perform during the year and an assessment task by task of how well or how badly he had performed. If there are valid factors, affecting the performance, these should be mentioned. This should be followed by space for comments on any obstacles to the man's better performance, and for comments on his career ambitions and training needs. This may be followed by a summary of the performance assessment and space for the man to sign that he has read and understood the review. There should be space for any confidential comments by the appraiser, including suggestions for promotion or alternative employment followed by his signature. Finally there should be space for the appraising manager's manager to comment. A good review form has a minimum of detailed headings and a maximum of space for writing comments.

It is quite a sound plan to have an action form on which to list all the actions agreed at the appraisal interview. This can act as a reminder for both manager and man.

The Review Procedure

A week or so before the appraisal interview is to take place, the man should be told that his performance is to be reviewed and an appointment made. He should at this stage be told briefly the purpose of the review, shown a blank copy of the review form and possibly given some explanatory notes, setting out the purpose of the review with a reminder that he should sort out his own ideas on the following before the appraisal interview:

1 His job description.
2 His own ideas on how he has performed against the objectives set.
3 Any special success or failure during the year.
4 What help he needs to improve performance.
5 What he thinks he himself can do to improve his performance.
6 How he sees his future career.
7 The sort of training he feels would help him to perform better in his current job and to forward his career.

Preparing for the Appraisal Interview

The manager must make some preparations for the interview. As with any staff interview, he must arrange to hold the interview in an office without interruptions. He should look out the man's job specification and check it over. He should also pencil out draft replies to the questions in the review form to guide him in the appraisal interview.

The Appraisal Interview

The appraisal interview should open with a restatement of the aims of the interview. The manager should emphasise the need for participation from the man being appraised and try to encourage a free and frank exchange. As the interview proceeds, each question on the form should be discussed, after which the manager writes down his answer. The man should see what is written. It is probably helpful to give him a blank copy of the form to have in front of him during the interview. Finally, at the end of the interview the man should be handed a copy of the form to read and sign. He may, even after discussion, not agree with your assessment of his performance. In a good review system there will be a procedure for appeal. If this is so in your company you should explain the appeal system to him. At this stage the agreed actions should be listed separately with a note of whether the action lies on man or manager. Some indication of the timescale for action should also be given. A copy of the action list should be given to the man, preferably there and then, but, if this is not possible, as soon as a copy can be made. The interview should then be closed. Performance review and appraisal systems are time consuming but organisations which have used them for some time are generally agreed that the time and effort is more than repaid in better performance.

The Appraisal Interview

It has been traditional in many annual reporting systems to concentrate on aspects of character and potential. We believe that what a manager is concerned with is whether or not his people are performing satisfactorily in their jobs. The fact that a man has deserted his wife, gets drunk every Saturday night or plays rugger for a good club is totally irrelevant unless it affects his performance in his job. Our prime purpose is to measure and then to reward a man's performance against his agreed objectives. The whole review and appraisal system must be simple enough for everyone concerned with it to understand what it is all about and for ordinary line managers to operate it as part of their job without having a personnel manager permanently in attendance to explain its ramifications.

The fact that you have an annual appraisal system does not mean that you do nothing about your people's performance during the rest of the year. You are, of course, always concerned about it. If you notice particularly effective work you should comment on it at the time. Similarly, if someone is performing badly, you should discuss the matter with him and try to agree what action is needed to pull performance back up to standard.

Rewards

Good performance against objectives set and agreed must be rewarded. There is nothing more stultifying to effort than a situation where a man knows that his salary increase for the year will bear no relation whatsoever to his performance to date. Such a situation is, however, commonplace for government service where strict pay scales exist. Civil servants have to possess that frame of mind to acknowledge such a system.

To obtain good morale in a work force and to produce the best performance from people, it is essential that performance be related to reward. A mediocre or poor performance must not in any circumstance be rewarded. Indeed poor performance must be succeeded by satisfactory performance within a limited time or the poor performer must be removed from his job. The rot can spread outwards quite quickly when someone who can plainly be seen not to be performing is not only not penalised but is seen to be as well rewarded as someone whose performance is wholly up to expectations.

In saying this we do not mean to imply that every mistake must be used to condemn the man who made it. We all make mistakes. One of the best ways of learning is by learning from our mistakes. The man who never makes a mistake is one who is dead sure of his facts before he acts and never takes a risk. He is never likely to go very far or achieve very much. We can learn from our mistakes and we can improve our judgement and our performance by learning from our mistakes. So don't be too hard on your people just because they make mistakes, provided they recognise that they have made a mistake, why they have made it and don't make the same mistake twice. Anyone can make a mistake once; only a fool makes the same mistake twice.

THE QUALITY OF MERCY

Poor performance cannot be tolerated and certainly must not be rewarded. Yet this does not mean we should be inhuman. Poor performance may be due to a number of reasons. It may be our fault for giving a man a job for which he is not suitable. We must not penalise him for our own failure. He may have been promoted to that level at which he performs incompetently. If this sounds unconvincing, it has been elaborated in a book, *The Peter Principle* (see Bibliography). It is also possible that a period of rapid change has left a man far behind. This is a particularly difficult case as it frequently happens to people who have given long and loyal service to an organisation, but who are no longer able to adapt to a period of rapid change. Their lack of performance in their current job cannot be tolerated, yet it would be callous to throw them on the dole queue after the company has had their services in their more productive years. A real attempt must be made to find a job for them where their strengths and abilities can be used productively. When someone is falling down on the job, it is easy to overlook his strengths and abilities. Yet they exist in all of us and it is certain that they exist in a considerable degree in people who have served your company well for many years. If there has been a real decline in capability with premature onset of old age or some other cause which makes him unsuitable for any productive job in the company, then he will have to go. He should in these circumstances be treated generously both as to pension and a golden handshake, if only because his colleagues are watching to see how he will be treated. Poor performance cannot be tolerated, but behind the poor performance lies a human being who must be understood and helped.

PROMOTION

One aspect of rewarding a job well done is promotion. Indeed in many fields there is an over-emphasis on promotion to the extent that many people come to look on their job as just one more rung in the promotion ladder. Much of the working population is still employed in large organisations which have a pyramid structure. Only one man sits at the very top and by the nature of a pyramid only a small proportion of people can expect to struggle more than a few rungs up the ladder. Constant emphasis on promotion as a form of reward leads to frustration on the part of those who do not get promotion. It also leads to good technical people accepting promotion into administrative and management posts for which they are not fitted.

So far as possible every job should be designed to be satisfying in itself. The system of financial reward in the company should be such that a good technical man can be seen to have a route upwards within his technical speciality. In some companies, for instance, a really top grade technician or professional man can move up a technical non-managerial ladder and perhaps reach the standing of a divisional manager with some such title as principal technical officer. He continues to work at his speciality, where he is of greatest value to the organisation. He is probably more content himself to follow his speciality, particularly because the organisation has the good sense to give him the status, seniority and salary which he earns.

Any formal salary scale should not just have a single fixed salary for the job. There should also be adequate room to allow a man who does the job superlatively well, but is unsuitable for promotion, to be adequately rewarded. The very top rate of pay for a job might, for instance, overlap the starting rate of pay for a job two grades up in the hierarchy.

SPECIAL EFFORT: SPECIAL REWARD

Large organisations are frequently obsessed with salary scales and frameworks to the extent that it becomes impossible to reward a man for special effort without promoting him. Special efforts should be recognised and rewarded. Most people can be persuaded to make an extra special effort once in order to help in achieving some objective. But, if there is no recognition or reward for the effort, it will be a lot harder to enlist their support a second time. The possibility of special one-off bonuses should not be overlooked.

THANKS

This is a small word but it helps a lot. In the last analysis people of course wish to receive a tangible reward in the shape of increased salary, perks or promotion. They do also and very much more immediately wish to be appreciated. They also want other people, particularly their colleagues, to see that they are appreciated. This is an area where a junior manager may play a large part. He may not be able to directly influence his company's salary policy. He can, however, make sure that where any of his people put up a good performance that it is recognised, and that he gets some praise and public recognition for it. Where somebody outside your department does something to help you, a letter of thanks to him or a letter to his manager drawing attention to the good work always helps to give people a feeling of satisfaction and a desire to help next time.

Where your people have performed exceptionally well, they will appreciate a reference to their contribution in published material. If appropriate a laudatory comment may be placed in the local paper or in a house journal. The divisional manager or some member of higher management may be persuaded on his next visit to stop and talk to the star performers and thank them for their good work. Among professional and technical staff the opportunity to attend meetings of professional associations in the firm's time is a reward, which is sometimes greatly appreciated.

Conclusion

However it is done your people must be rewarded for their performance against the objectives set them in their current job. Whatever the limitations imposed by the company's personnel and salary policy, the manager must keep this basic principle in the forefront of his mind.

nine Taking over Existing Staff

The New Manager

Sometimes when a manager is first appointed to a job, he will be properly inducted into it. He will meet his new senior manager, who will discuss the job with him and say what he expects. The senior manager will introduce him to his predecessor and there will be an adequate handover period. Depending upon the job this handover period could range from a couple of days to several weeks.

Unfortunately we do not live in a perfect world. It is just as likely that you will simply be told that you have been appointed manager of the blanket section from next Monday morning. The man who appoints you knows what the blanket section is and what it does. There's always been a blanket section in the firm—everyone knows what it is and does. The possibility that you don't doesn't enter anyone's head. If you want the job, you have to face the blanket section on Monday morning and manage it. Before you can manage it you will need to find out where it is, why it exists, what it does and how it does it and, most important, who are the people who form the blanket section. We are concerned in this chapter with coming to grips with the people.

The Existing Staff

Most people find the unknown frightening. One of the most difficult aspects of taking on a new job as a manager is coming to grips with the existing staff. They know each other, they know the job and the rules. They will tend to take up a defensive attitude in the face of their new and unknown manager. He is new and unknown even if he has been promoted from within the section or branch. He is new because, whether or not he recognises it, he is no longer just one of the boys. He, or she, is now the leader to whom the others will turn for direction or guidance. He has to deal with the problems and non-standard situations. It is he who must carry full responsibility for the performance of the section. So although the emphasis may vary, any new manager taking over a job with existing staff has certain problems to face and certain tasks to achieve. He has to get to know the staff, their capabilities, their shortcomings and their potential; has to establish in them a feeling of confidence in his ability both to do the job and to look after their interests; he has to persuade them to devote their minds, interest and energy to their job. This is true whether he has been appointed from the section, transferred in from elsewhere in the company, come from another company or been appointed directly from school, college or university.

Improvements

When taking over existing staff, it is always wise to take some time to discover the form before you start altering the existing arrangements and method of doing the job. On the first morning people may come to you with plausible ideas for improving things: if only we did so and so how much better it would be. Be wary. It may be a genuinely sensible suggestion, which can bring a marked improvement in the results achieved by the section. It can also be someone trying to settle an old score or trying to land you in trouble. Whichever it may be, give yourself time to consider it. Listen to the suggestion, probe it gently and promise to consider it. Explain that although it seems a good suggestion to you, that you want to find out how the whole section works and fits into the company as a whole before you make any changes. This gives you a breathing space to find out if it really is a good suggestion or just a trap. Don't forget the suggestion or who made it. You must come back to him in the course of the next few days to tell him what you have decided to do about his suggestion.

Your Notebook

There will be a lot of things you have to remember in the course of your new job. Many of them are things which people tell you and they will be offended if you forget them. If not offended, they will realise and resent the fact that your interest in them is superficial. Your interest in your people must neither be superficial nor appear to be superficial. Some people have excellent memories for detail though most of us don't. In most cases it is helpful to keep a notebook. One of the most important uses of the manager's notebook is for him to keep full and confidential notes on his staff. This part of the notebook forms the record of his human inventory.

In large companies, personnel departments keep, as a matter of course, records of every employee with a personal file containing a copy of every letter from, to or about the employee since he first applied to join the firm. Some extract or summary sheet containing bare details about the man is almost certainly provided to some level of line management. It may well not be provided to the lowest levels of line management. Even if it is provided you still need your own notebook. The mere fact that you compile it laboriously in your own hand helps to imprint the contents in your mind and also allows you to record the facts which you consider important. Secondly, the fact that you carry it in your pocket means that you always have it available when you want it: perhaps at home in the evening or during illness; perhaps on a visit to another part of the company or when with one of its customers or suppliers; perhaps when you are at a management meeting and are asked whether you have someone available with a particular aptitude.

The manager's notebook is a key tool and should be constructed as quickly as possible after he is appointed to a job. Thereafter he will keep it up to date as circumstances change. The section dealing with people will be in two parts. First, he needs a summary, showing how his human inventory relates to budget. Second, he needs an individual record of every person who works for him.

The Individual Personal Record

It is simplest to consider these individual records first. The layout depends on personal choice and on the size and shape of the notebook which will fit convenient into the manager's suit pocket or handbag, as the case may be. The heading information is straightforward factual information, which should be available from the company's personnel records or from the previous holder of your job. This information covers: full name, address and telephone number (if any), whether married or single, date of birth, date of joining company, salary, with date and size of last two salary increases, details of any special allowances or expenses payable, e.g. for some special qualification or for running a car, formal qualifications, e.g. number of 'O' levels or other educational and technical qualifications, title of job.

After these basic items, the remainder becomes a matter of choice and is gradually built up from odd snippets of information picked up over the months. More personal details are useful. For young people: do they live at home? if not, what is the name and address of their parent or guardian? For married people: do they have children? of what age? are they at school or university or at work? does the husband or wife work and, if so, where? For older people: the name and address of their next of kin and comment about any health troubles. For all his staff: their hobbies and outside interests.

It may seem that all this information is of no concern to the manager. It is personal information and he is just nosey parkering in trying to secure it. Certainly he should not appear to be prying when it is obtained. Most of it will come to him just by listening. Most people like to talk about themselves. They will talk during breaks, in the canteen over lunch and when they are packing up to go home. On top of that quite a lot of personal chat will come out in the course of normal working discussions. The information is important to you in your job. It helps you to understand your people. When a married woman becomes a late arriver, looks perpetually worried and is not doing her work properly it will help you to deal with her in an understanding way and to bring her back on course, if you know that she is keen for her only son to have a good education and that he has been subjected to an important examination a few weeks back.

On the whole, most people do not do poor work from sheer bloody-mindedness. They work badly because they are misplaced in their job, because they are mismanaged or because for some reason they are unhappy or unsettled. The unhappiness may be caused by something totally unconnected with work. Nonetheless it affects the quality of the work performed just as surely as an unhappiness arising from the working situation. If you have some idea of the cause of their unhappiness, however vague, it will almost certainly help you in bringing them back to full productivity.

The facts in these personal records also help you in the occasional situation where immediate action is needed as in the case of illness or accident at work. No doubt the personnel officer would sort it out all in due course, but your notebook can help you to take immediate action.

Finally the personal record should contain information about the training each person has had and comments about their abilities, aptitudes and interests. The facts that someone can type even though it is not part of their normal job may be useful on some occasion when typing is urgently needed in order to get a letter into the post, after the typists have left the office. An interest in the Red Cross and first aid is a more obvious example of the sort of thing that it can be useful to know of. A man or woman's outside interests can often be used to the benefit of the company on some occasion if they are known about. The sort of outside interest we have seen put to good account are amateur interests in photography, flower arranging, local history and topography, do-it-yourself, painting, drawing and all sorts of private interests in the electrical, mechanical and radio fields. A man or woman may be an amateur in the sense that their interest is pursued in their spare time but may nonetheless be an expert. Not only are their abilities and depth of knowledge frequently as good as full time workers in the field, they are usually flattered to be called on from time to time to exercise their skill.

Apart from any possible relevance to the immediate job in hand, the range of outside interests of outwardly quite ordinary people is staggering. Many run their interests almost as a part-time business and may make a substantial income from it. Over the years in the factories and offices in which we have worked we have come across the following: a man who ran a small Christmas tree plantation; a part-time rally driver; breeders of dogs, cats and donkeys; a man who ran a village store; another who operated a part-time insurance agency; a man who translated foreign technical documents from French and another from Russian; people who glide, sail, pilot fixed wing aircraft; embryo poets and novelists; people who take part in local government; belong to local societies; sit on school and hospital boards and take part in other forms of voluntary work. These interests, we emphasise, are followed by quite ordinary men and women, not wealthy people but ordinary people working for their living in ordinary occupations.

Don't Run a Gossip Shop

In some of their hobbies or interests, people may want some special consideration at work. It may help them to leave half an hour early on the first Tuesday in each month, for instance, to go to a committee meeting. If there is a good reason behind it, be sympathetic to such requests, providing the work is still done effectively

70

and on time. It helps to make the people concerned contented in their work and ties them more firmly to the company. Their outside interest may have no direct relevance to their job, but it broadens their outlook. You cannot begin to understand people unless you know about their interests. Most people like to talk about their hobby. The fact that they can talk to you about it helps to create a bond of understanding between you. However, this comes not in a day or two but over a period of months or years. One word of warning: you are not running a gossip shop. Watch that these discussions are kept to the appropriate times and not allowed to last too long. As has been said, when discussing the use of your own time, aimless gossip can run away with a disproportionate amount of your day. Nonetheless management is people and people take time. Some part of this time is legitimately spent in getting to know about them by listening to them. There should also be a note of their weaknesses. The fact that you keep your notebook in your own handwriting in your own pocket means that it is one of the very few documents which really is confidential and for your eyes alone. Everybody has some weaknesses and it will save a lot of regrets if you recognise from the start that your people, like everyone else, have weaknesses.

A major reason for recognising weaknesses and strengths in your staff is so that this knowledge can be applied in improving the work of your section. One man may be quite incapable of adding up a row of figures and getting the right answer. In days gone by some members of the BF and BI management would deliberately have given such a man as much work involving addition of figures work as possible. This would be done to let him know who was master or for the good of his soul. The consequence would be that the man was miserable, his work output low and the working atmosphere would deteriorate. Modern managers will try to help their staff to overcome their weaknesses but will concentrate on harnessing each man's strengths to the job while trying to avoid relying on his performance in the areas of his weakness. There is considerable wisdom in the old Stock Exchange saying that you should cut your losses and run your profits. This applies to people as much as to stocks and shares.

Be Objective

As you fill up the individual sheets of your notebook try to be as objective as possible. Try not to be influenced by your prejudices. You may not like tall girls or men with beards but these dislikes

71

are totally irrelevant and must not be allowed to influence your judgements. We all have prejudices; it is best to recognise your own and specifically offset them in making your judgements. More seriously, it is essential to avoid discrimination against certain categories of people on grounds of religion, politics, sex, race or age.

As you are getting to know the existing staff of the section and you should be looking out for the informal organisation pattern. What are the links between people inside and outside the section which make things happen and the links down which information flows? Which of your staff have lunch together? Who have common interests or club memberships? Who is courting whom? And which beautiful friendships have become unstuck in the past and left sour feelings behind? An understanding of these links may explain many things which happen in the section and which are otherwise inexplicable.

The Notebook Summary

As well as the individual sheets about each person in your note-book, you will also need a summary. This should list the budgeted staff of the section by grade or job title and show how actual staff present match the budget both by numbers and by salary. Depending on the company or the type of work the section is doing it may be desirable to split budget and actual figures in some other way, e.g. by subsection or class of work or experience level of the people. The choice depends upon what is meaningful in your particular context. Whatever the choice, it must serve as a reminder of things which need your attention, e.g. staff recruitment that is needed. Another useful part of this summary section is a note of the company salary scales for the types of staff in your section; notes on admissible rates of expenses if this is applicable to your section; notes on holiday entitlements and a sheet showing holidays for each person in the current year.

Establish Yourself with Your People

When you take over a section of existing staff, one of the things you have to do is to establish their confidence in you as a manager. An effective way of starting on this is to discover what are the minor irritations which impede the section in their work or make life uncomfortable for them. Having done this, try to find a way of overcoming some or all of these problems. For instance, the girls may complain that the towels in the ladies' lavatories are only changed once a week on Monday mornings and are filthy by Tuesday lunch time. Find out who is responsible and chase after them to have the towels changed three times a week. Push hard at it. Nobody will want to know, but it is somebody's job to see that there are clean towels. Find out who it is and give them no peace till they perform satisfactorily. Every section has its minor irritations and a great many of them can be cured if the manager cares enough to find out who is responsible, to suggest how an improvement can be made and to keep after the person responsible until the improvement is made. One thing every body of people wants in their manager is the ability to get things done. Let your section see as soon as possible that you get things done, even if to start with they are quite minor things. There will be no need to brag about it to them. They will recognise your performance even more certainly than you will recognise theirs.

Dealing with the Passengers

When you take over any sizeable section, the chances are that you will find some passengers—people who have just come along for the ride and are not pulling their weight. Try to discover why they are not pulling their weight and try to persuade them to a better performance. The techniques referred to in the previous chapter will help with this. Among the passengers may well be a hopeless case, an elderly widow who is quite incapable of doing any job properly for instance. Be very patient and careful with such people. They may be alone in the world; they may have some other person completely dependent on them and on their earnings. Your company is not a charitable organisation dispensing social security benefits, but it is—if you work for it—humane in its relationships with such people. If they are sacked, they may never get another job and merely deteriorate unproductively drawing State benefits. Common humanity demands that you lean over backwards to encourage and help such people to do their work. Remember that everyone has some strong points. Try to find such strong points and if necessary reorganise the work of the section to allow this person to make her contribution to the section's performance. Although the rest of the section may complain bitterly about her, they are also likely to be all on her side if you procure her sacking. Such action may adversely affect section morale and attitudes with a consequent fall in the standard of performance.

If your feeling of common humanity does not run very deep

and if you are dedicated to absolute efficiency judged in money terms, pause. Recognise that in the medium term your job will probably be done more effectively and more easily if you act considerately in all your dealings with your people. It is not just being soft for it pays in results. Remember that management is people.

ten Recruiting New Staff

A Management Opportunity

The recruitment of new staff presents an opportunity for every manager. Care and thought in recruitment enables him to improve the performance of his section, cover some of the weaknesses or gaps in the section's abilities and also provide the human basis for the execution of his future plans. When you take over an existing section you have little option but to take the people as you find them and do your best to improve their performance. With new staff the position is entirely different, as you should make every effort to make sure you get the best person available for the job in question. In some companies there may be a tendency to leave recruitment to the personnel department who will provide a clerk, a graduate, a programmer with COBOL experience, a typist or an HNC electrical engineer on demand. This is not good enough. So far as circumstances allow, you should insist on having a say in the choice of new staff for your section, not only having a say but an opportunity to go over the applicants' papers and of interviewing a selection of the more promising candidates.

Before any recruitment is started you will have to define the job that is to be done and the sort of person you want to fill it. You will also have to obtain approval in principle to recruiting to fill the vacancy. This may be a mere formality if it is a replacement for someone who is leaving or if budget provision has been made for an extra person in your plans for this year. However, for a totally new job you will probably have to seek the approval of your own manager. This may initially be given informally in discus-

75

sion of your current work or future plans. Alternately you may have plans for improving the effectiveness of your section. These will have been formalised into a document setting out the nature of your proposals, the benefits which you expect to accrue to the company if the plan is implemented and a plan for implementation of the proposals. This plan will set out any organisational changes involved, any additional staff required, a timetable and a statement of costs.

Is External Recruitment Necessary?

Whether such a formal proposal is required or not, considerable thought must be given to the matter before recruitment is initiated. First, what is the job to be done? If Mr Plume, the chief clerk of subsection A gives in his notice, the easy way out is to say you need a replacement chief clerk for subsection A. This on the face of it is the quickest and easiest way of filling a routine but busy job. However, it is passing-up an opportunity. It may also be the first reaction of a harassed and over-worked section manager, but it would be the wrong one. The opportunity should be taken to examine Mr Plume's job and those with which it interacts. Is the job really necessary? This may seem a ridiculous question to ask when Plume gets in early every morning, has his head down all day and moves a mountain of paper every day. Now is, however, a good time to ask the question when there are no overtones of redundancy to cloud the discussion. Careful examination may reveal that hard though Mr Plume works, his real contribution to the objectives of your section may be slight. Careful scrutiny may show that subsections A and B can be united under one chief clerk, while each clerk in the combined subsection undertakes a little bit more responsibility in his own area.

Maybe it will turn out that Plume's job is essential, so you carefully revise the job specification to see that it is up to date. The next step is to consider the sort of person who is required to do it. Once the qualities required have been listed, you are ready to set about filling the job. The first place to look is within your own section; is there anyone fit for promotion to fill the job? If there is, well and good; if not the next stage is to consider whether anyone can be found inside the company. The problem should be briefly discussed with your own manager in case he wishes to transfer or promote someone from one of his other sections. Next the personnel officer should be consulted.

Your company may have a plan for rotating staff between

different parts of the company or it may be so rigidly compart-mentalised that staff rarely move across the well defined depart-mental boundaries. Other companies run schemes for the internal advertising of vacancies in the company newspaper or house journal and on the company notice boards. However it is organised, you should try to see if anyone is available internally. By doing this, it may be possible to absorb someone from another depart-ment which is being reduced in size. The company does not have to incur the costs of recruitment and these are considerable both in hard cash for advertising, agency costs and interview expenses and also in indirect costs which are largely your time. Furthermore someone recruited internally should require less training than a new recruit. He should know a certain amount about the company, its organisation and products. Training of an internal recruit should be just a topping up process dealing largely with the particular nature of the job he is to do.

Internal Recruiting Dangers

However, there are snags with internal recruiting. Once you have put the process in motion, it may prove difficult to reject some-one who you think does not quite fit the bill. You may also be subject to pressure to accept someone who is not right for the job. Some managers are not prepared to face up to sacking people who ought to be sacked or dealing with people who have been over-promoted. Their way out is to try to arrange internal trans-fers, thus passing their problem on to some other manager. A variation of this is the manager who passes on his troublemakers. The troublemakers range from those who ought to be sacked—the man who consistently arrives very late in the morning and comes back from lunch drunk every afternoon—to the person who is just a nuisance, for example the malicious gossip. You must do your utmost to avoid being landed with these duds and troublemakers. Don't be content with studying the papers. A poor manager will not only try to pass on his problems, he will also cover up when writing reports on staff. Even an interview may not show up the trouble. In the case of internal transfers, it is always wise to try to glean some information informally by tactful inquiries from your acquaintances in the company; in other words check on the grapevine.

Another possible problem with internal recruiting is the 'relative'. If you are offered the company secretary's daughter on transfer from elsewhere in the company, where she is considered suitable, and you turn her down, you are in danger of making an enemy at the centre of the company. Yet if you take her on and she is incompetent you will be in an even worse predicament. This, like many other problems, is best tackled as soon as it appears. If she seems to you after careful consideration to be unsuitable for the job, turn her down as tactfully as possible: perhaps the job will not offer sufficient scope and interest for someone of her ability and intelligence!

Recruitment Procedure

If there is no suitable candidate for the job from inside the company, external recruiting will be necessary. The routine of this will be handled by your personnel officer. It is probably best to see him or her for a preliminary discussion. Take along a copy of the job description and a profile of the sort of person you are looking for. This profile should give the qualifications and attributes for which you are looking, the salary for the job, the probable age range of the candidate and an indication of whether you are looking for someone with potential for development. The personnel officer will indicate how he hopes to bring in candidates, from an agency, from personal contact with local schools, technical colleges or university or from a special or general advertisement in the press. If it is to be by a special advertisement, you should help to draft it. Certainly make sure you see the final draft before it goes to the newspaper.

Whatever the source of the external recruitment, the personnel office will in due course pass you a number of letters and/or forms of application for the job, possibly with some comment on their suitability. The applications should be studied carefully. The way in which they have been completed will tell you quite a lot about a person. For a clerical job it shows whether the applicant can do tidy work. For someone who has to write reports or write to customers, it should show if he can express himself simply, clearly and concisely. In many more subtle ways, what the applicant chooses to say about himself and the way he says it will give you a clue to the sort of person he is. Even what he has obviously left out is important. Apart from such indications it gives you all the facts about the man. The application form and letter are unlikely to tell you which is the right man for the job, but it will tell you who should be rejected out of hand and who should be called in for interview.

Preparing for the Job Interview

Whether a job is to be filled from internal or external recruitment, applicants will have to be interviewed. Interviewing job applicants is a key management task, which is undertaken by all levels of management. Even the chairman or managing director of the largest companies have to handle such interviews, if only when filling jobs such as managing directorships of subsidiaries. In their case the interviews are probably not formally job applicant selection interviews since they will have been carried out discreetly over the months or years as succession planning goes on. Job applicant interviewing, at whatever level, is important. As soon as possible in your first management post you should start to get experience of this vital task. Apart from interviewing to fill your own vacancies, there may be other opportunities. In some expanding companies, as part of their general recruitment campaign, they may offer informal interviews to people in a particular town or centre on one or more evenings. The interviews are advertised in the local and national or trade press. They are generally for special staff in short supply such as programmers or certain types of engineer. The interviews are carried out informally to see whether the people who come in might be suitable for the company and, if they might be, then to encourage them to proceed with an application to join. Such interviews are generally carried out by a mixture of personnel staff and line managers. Frequently the personnel department find difficulty in persuading line managers to undertake an extra evening commitment of this kind. They welcome volunteers, and this may prove a good first opportunity to try your hand at interviewing.

Before you start interviewing you must prepare for it. The circumstances of the interview must be such that the applicant can relax his guard sufficiently for you to learn something of the real person. Your preparations must be aimed at making this possible. Enough time must be allowed for the interview. In most cases a thorough job cannot be done under three-quarters of an hour and this should be free from disturbance from visitors, phone calls or the demands of your secretary or other staff. If you have a secretary, she must be briefed to prevent interruptions. If you haven't, then at the least you should put a 'Do not disturb' notice on the door and tell the switchboard to intercept your phone calls. It is probably preferable to do the interviewing in your own office. If this is not possible it should be in some place where privacy is possible. The applicant should not be distracted by what is going on around him nor should he feel that he can be overheard by staff working nearby. The ideal is clearly a properly closed off office and not one corner of a large modern open plan area. Needless to say the interview room/office should be clean, tidy, well lit, adequately heated and ventilated. Even if you do not smoke, have a clean ashtray in the room. If the applicant smokes, it may help to put him at his ease. If your office administration makes it possible make arrangements for two cups of coffee or tea to be brought in at the beginning of the interview. This also helps to break the ice. Needless to say you should also have refreshed your memory about the job specification, the profile of the person you are looking for and the conditions of service—hours of work, amount of holiday, salary, etc—which can be offered for the job. The letters of application and application form should be carefully studied and the key points noted; nothing is more irritating to the applicant than an interviewer, who by his questions and conversations shows he has not read the application form, which has probably been compiled laboriously and with great care.

Some junior managers have been known to carry on an interview with their desk top littered with papers of all shapes and sizes, constantly breaking off the interview to take phone calls, and dispensing a succession of instant decisions on trivial matters to a constant stream of interrupters. They believe they are giving an impression of the high powered troubleshooting executive. They are not; the impression they give is that of an incompetent little man, who is out of his depth.

The Seven-Point Plan

When you are interviewing someone, do not forget that the interview has a purpose: to enable you to assess whether the applicant is suitable to appoint to the vacancy you are trying to fill. A secondary purpose is for the applicant to decide whether he wants to accept the job if it is offered to him. How do you set about assessing the applicant. One way, which we have found effective is to carry on the interview with a view to reaching an assessment of the person on seven key points. Some of these points are more critical than others, but they are all relevant to your decision. The seven points are dealt with in some detail.

1 SUPERFICIAL

Some assessment of a person can be made on the basis of his appearance, bearing and speech. This should not be an exercise period for your personal prejudices about hair or style of dress. However, the objective needs of the job should be borne in mind. For instance, at the time of writing, a young man appearing at an interview for a job as a capital goods salesman in the UK or Europe who chose to wear a kaftan at the interview is likely to be unsuitable. Apart from the suitability of that form of dress for such a salesman, his appearance would throw doubt on his desire to get the job and also on his judgement.

Quite a lot can be guessed about a man or woman from their appearance. Anyone applying for a job should and probably will be neat, clean and tidy. Some will be dressed in the height of fashion, men as well as girls. Others will be dressed more conventionally. But it is worth noticing if a man has buttons missing from his shirt or jacket, dandruff on his collar or down at heel shoes. Are a girl's stockings/tights laddered, baggy or crooked, has she loose hairs on her shoulder, if she wears make-up has it been carefully or sloppily applied? When the applicant comes in does he appear serene, nervous or over-confident? Does he stand and walk upright or is he round shouldered and stooping? When he sits down, does he sit relaxed and comfortable, lean on your desk, slouch in the chair or sit nervously on the edge of the chair. Does he talk to you or to the floor or to some distant object? Is his speech clear or blurred, pleasant or grating, easy or difficult to understand?

In days gone by a great many interviews were decided purely on such a superficial assessment. Modern managers assess applicants under this heading, but it is only one of seven headings and not by any means the most important.

2 ATTAINMENTS

In most walks of life, we try to predict the future to a large extent from our knowledge of the past and our guesses about how past patterns will be repeated or modified by changing circumstances. So an important part of our assessment is to look at what the applicant's attainments are. What has he achieved in the past? This must be related to the person's age and opportunities. A school leaver's attainments will be limited to his achievements in school examinations, his sports and hobbies, whereas a man of forty will be expected to have some solid achievements behind him in his working life. Some weight in this assessment must be given to the opportunity for achievement, difficult though this is to judge. For instance, in judging 18 year olds we would give greater weight to the one who failed the 11+, went to a secondary modern school and obtained two 'A' levels, than we would to one who went to a leading grammar or public school and obtained several 'A' levels. The first we assume has overcome early failure and has succeeded in the face of considerable difficulty, indicating some persistence and determination. The second undoubtedly has an achievement to his credit, but one which has probably been achieved more easily and certainly in less difficult circumstances. Generally speaking you want to recruit effective people. It is a hard fact of life that some people are more effective in getting results than others. There are some non-achievers, who always have an excuse for failure. The excuses are full and plausible, but beware of them.

3 INTELLIGENCE

Different jobs require different levels of intelligence. No one seems to be too sure what intelligence is anyway. We may be looking for someone with a reasonable amount of nous or common sense. For the majority of clerical, administrative and supervisory posts, this is basically what we are seeking under the heading of intelligence. Some indication can be obtained from the way in which the applicant appreciates and answers your questions. For technical and professional staff some indication that they have the necessary intelligence for the level of job can be adduced from their qualifications and from the way in which they discuss their speciality and past experience.

4 APTITUDES

In drawing up the profile of the person required to fill the vacancy, you will have listed certain aptitudes as being essential and others merely desirable. Some aptitudes are necessarily difficult to judge at an interview. If, for instance, you are going to take on trainee or junior computer programmers, you will almost certainly want them to be given an aptitude test before you interview them and will have the results in front of you when you do the interview. An aptitude for self-expression or artistic aptitudes may be more easily recognised in the interview itself.

5 INTERESTS

You may aim to find out the applicants interests. These may range from TV watching, playing the violin, dancing, painting to rugger

82

playing or social work. You cannot make a valid judgement of a person without having an idea of his interests in life. It is generally an encouraging sign to find that people have a creative interest of some sort or that they play an active rather than a passive role in some field.

6 DISPOSITION

What sort of person is he? Will he get on with the other people in the section? Will he have the right personal characteristics to deal with people outside the section and if applicable with customers or suppliers? Is he apparently ambitious? Is he likely to accept responsibility? How suitable does he appear to be in disposition for this job?

7 CIRCUMSTANCES

What are his personal circumstances and how are they likely to affect his performance in this job? Is he married or single? Has he children or other dependants? Has he strong ties in the local area: of family, schooling or membership of local clubs and societies? Is he prepared to travel for the company if need be? This divides down into short trips and long trips, travel at home or abroad? Is he prepared to move and settle elsewhere?

This may seem a formidable list of inquiries. Not every question will necessarily be relevant for the job which you are trying to fill. However, for almost every job there is something of concern under each of the seven points. Before the interview you should go over the job specification and the personal profile. List under the seven points the things which you think are of importance for this job. Also put down the weighting for this job that you give to each of the seven points. For instance for a junior secretary a fairly high rating is likely to be given to superficial, intelligence, aptitudes and disposition and fairly low to the other three. For a maintenance man to keep the boilers and heating system going not a great deal of weight will be attached to the superficial points nor to his interests or circumstances. Nonetheless, they will have some bearing on how he does his job.

The Interview

After all this preparation, it is perhaps time to settle down to the interview itself. Don't keep the applicant hanging around, when he arrives; if he has to wait because he has arrived far too early make sure he has somewhere comfortable to wait. Provide something for him to read, preferably something about the company or its products. Collect him yourself from the reception area and take him to the interview room. Relieve him of his overcoat, umbrella, etc, and sit him down. The first task is to put him at ease as quickly as possible. A cup of tea or coffee at the beginning of the interview is a great help, but do make sure it is hot and in a clean unchipped cup. Don't forget that the applicant is summing you and the company up just as much as you are summing him up. In starting the interview look for something in the application form on which to base a question which will start him off talking to you naturally, preferably something about one of his declared interests. From this you can lead into a conversation, in which you lead him to tell you the things you need to know. This is the main reason why a good interview takes such a long time. The basic information might be obtainable from a series of questions with yes/no answers, but this really gives you very little idea of the applicant beyond that obtainable from his application form and appearance. Try to avoid this type of interview. A free two-way conversation will flow more easily and you will discover things which might otherwise have eluded you. You will also see him more nearly as he will eventually be at work.

As well as obtaining information about the applicant, you have to tell him about the company and the job so that he can judge whether or not he wants to work for the company and whether the job is one that he wants. This is probably best done after the applicant has talked to you about himself, his past and his hopes for the future. After you have told him about the company and the job, give him an opportunity to ask questions. You can learn quite a lot about someone from the questions he asks. In this part of the interview, you are in effect selling the company and the job to the applicant. Whether or not you eventually offer him the job and whether or not he accepts it, you want him to go away believing that your company is a good one. He may talk to other people, both possible future job applicants and the company's customers. The impression you want him to give them is a favourable one. However, don't fall into the trap of overselling either the company or the job.

When describing the conditions of employment be factual and do not be tempted to promise more than you can in fact offer. Even worse, don't give half promises. If the man joins you on the basis of half promises which are not fulfilled, you will in due course have a disgruntled and unhappy man working for you. You are unlikely to go wrong on the main item of salary. Watch that he does not join you under the impression that he will have a private office if in fact it will be an office shared with three others. Don't build up a picture of a marvellous canteen, if in fact it is a scruffy little room in which pork pies and sandwiches can be bought. Try to keep a sense of perspective in describing the company and its advantages. As well as mentioning any special benefits such as Luncheon Vouchers or free tea in the afternoon break, be careful to mention any rules which could later make difficulty: examples are rules relating to dress, for instance that overalls will be worn or that he will be expected to wear a white collar with a dark suit. There is no need to overstress it, but if it is a rule mention it. If staff are expected to work overtime without payment, be certain to mention it. Although such practices are still quite common, there are wide variations in practice. Specific points which you must cover are salary, fringe benefits, if any, pension scheme including when the man may join it, whether any removal expenses will be paid on taking up the job, the place of work, the working hours, holidays and a description of the job.

For somebody to whom you have decided to make an offer, it is quite a good move to show him round the place where he will work and for him to meet the people with whom he will work. Probably the best idea is to introduce him to one of your people with or for whom he will work and get him to show him round. This also gives the applicant a chance to ask a few more questions rather less formally and enables him to get a feel of the working atmosphere.

Closing the Interview

When you are ready to complete the interview, you should consider the next step. If the decision to employ the man lies with you and if you have firmly decided to offer the job, it is probably desirable to say that you or the personnel officer will send him a formal offer of employment in the course of the next few days. If on the other hand further interviews will be necessary, for example with your manager, you should try to arrange for this interview to be done before the applicant leaves.

Another point to be cleared before he leaves is that he should be offered and paid his travelling expenses for coming to the interview. In most cases they are probably only a few pence and the job applicant may be too nervous to ask for them himself. It is mean not to pay them and creates a very bad impression of the company. Finally, make sure that he gets back his coat and other belongings and is shown off the premises. Afterwards return the papers to the personnel department with your assessment and decision and check that they actually send a letter turning the man down or offering him the job.

eleven Communication

We may not often stop and think about both the magic and the evil of communication. It's magic when it's good, clean and satisfactory to all involved. It's evil when it's used to distort men's minds contrary to accepted standards of goodness, cleanliness or decency. Hot wars, cold wars and the aftermath show some of the evils. Away from the evil, however; let's talk about business communication which although one of its facets may be to alter people's minds from a course of action they may have previously accepted is still within the ethical environment of a normal business community.

What is Communication?

In the sense we are talking about it means a mutual exchange of thoughts between people. The thoughts may generate facts or opinions or be motivated by emotion. Communication occurs in all our social, business or political lives. As far as business is concerned, if we want value for money, communication must be very purposeful and to be effective we want the response we planned.

GROWTH OF COMMUNICATION

When we consider the wonder of the growth of communication closely coupled to the generation and availability of information we have a tremendous choice of media and subjects. We started communication in early man probably by gestures and went on to grunts and groans. (Some people still seem to grunt and groan!)

In what seems a short time in historical terms we progressed to an alphabet, printing, telegraph, radio, television, satellite and. . . .

TYPES OF COMMUNICATION

All methods must finally slot into the basic forms:

Speaking.
Writing.
Visual.
Gestures.
Listening.

We have not yet come very close to direct joining of minds for communication, but no doubt the silent treatment of a strike breaker or the silence of a cross girl friend are very close to mental communication even if apparently just nothing is being communicated!

Most of you may have heard the story of the other kind of communication, the indirect or by implication kind. The story is about the skipper of a ship who put in his log: 'The mate was drunk again last night.' The mate happening to see the entry thought he could get his own back and wrote: 'The captain was sober last night.'

You might have read this story dressed up in other ways, but silly as it may be it is a powerful example of communication by implication. Many advertisements use similar techniques: our so and so powder does not give you rashes, eat your arm away or slowly kill you, as though all the other powders do.

In communication, gestures are very important. If someone has suffered, a comforting arm round the shoulder is often better than a hundred times of 'I'm sorry'. Most of us use gestures a lot, the raised eyebrow, the thumbs up, the pointed finger and others we perhaps had better not mention. We'll talk some more in this chapter about writing and speaking, but visual communication is a very interesting case. It is valuable as a means of saving words, 'A picture is worth 10,000 words,' but it also can convey, in a flash, entirely wrong information unless the picture is carefully created. In communicating with our own management, the graph, bar chart or other picture is very useful, providing it really is conveying the message we want to give. Extra care, therefore, is needed in picture communication.

LISTENING

Listening was on the list of methods and communication could not exist without somebody listening. In fact intelligent and concentrated listening is vital to business communication. In industrial relations, for example, all parties must above all listen with the greatest care. We all fall foul of two important problems in listening. Firstly we think we've heard it all before when in fact we've heard only a bit of it before, but immediately we think 'We've heard it all before,' our mind shuts off the acuteness and concentration of our listening and we may miss an important new point hidden in what is now just a drone of conversation. The second danger is convincing ourselves that what is being said means something quite different. We could be said to be unreasonable; we are not really listening. This assumes of course that the sender is not sending such a garbled message that it is impossible to understand. This question of not really listening nearly always occurs when two parties have quite different interests or because the scene has been wrongly set by one of the communicators. Because industrial relations often provide good examples of this we spoke to a works manager friend of ours about the subject. He quoted several instances and was quick to point out he was far from perfect, but was attempting to learn the art of listening as fast as he could. The first thing he did emphasise was that listening must include the asking of questions to clarify points made or include the restatement of issues in your own words to check with the other person whether this was as he meant it to be received. He told us that one of his foremen had told a worker that his machine was dirty and 'to clean it up'. The man had resented this and before long they were arguing hammer and tongs about everything bar the dirty machine. They both had adopted attitudes, were not really listening to each other, but were much more interested in simply arguing. The manager happened to hear them and quickly calmed down both people. The problem was really this. The foreman quite rightly was not going to have a dirty machine because dirtiness was often a prelude to danger. It was not just plain 'bull'. Unfortunately the worker had not been on this particular machine for most of the time and couldn't manage to explain to the foreman that he felt it was a bit unjust. Their points of view could not be reconciled. They were not listening. The foreman should not have persisted in the argument, much better to have listened and found out what the real grievance was.

Effective Communication

As a manager the importance of effective communication can hardly be over-emphasised. It is undoubtedly a major task of every manager and directly affects all working relationships.

If a manager cannot communicate properly he cannot possibly either hope to get the best out of his own staff or be able to interpret and influence higher management. Another aspect is the effect on his own and his company image every time he writes, telephones or appears in public or at meetings. There is no shortage of reasons for the need to communicate effectively.

In general terms communication effectiveness depends on how credible the sender is to the receiver, since the receiver usually ascribes a motive to the message:

> Success of the message is more likely if it is supporting a belief already held.
> A communication that is repetitive or has a prolonging influence, in that it gives information little by little, is often more effective.
> In detail, short sentences with familiar words and active verbs make a communication interesting and persuasive.

Obstacles to Communication

To understand how to communicate properly involves understanding the obstacles and there is no shortage of these either! One of the biggest obstacles that also sets the scene for many others is consciously or unconsciously refusing to see the point of view of the other man or group of men. We say consciously as there is no doubt that some people are obstinate from a purely political point of view. Unconsciously refusing to see is very common. To provide a core of ideas or obstacles for you to expand we list some common ones below:

PREJUDICE This comes from deep-seated beliefs often stemming from personal experience or the experience of family or close friends. It can also arise from a lack of intelligence or wish not to learn, in a general sense.

WRONG TIME OR PLACE This is often unfortunate for a person with a good idea. He cannot seem to communicate it to others for many complex, unidentifiable reasons. Yet some short time afterwards, perhaps, the same audience is told the same thing by someone else and action commences straightaway. There is no clever answer to the wrong time or place obstacle, except to try to measure the receptivity before telling all.

TOO COMPLEX This is a fairly straightforward obstacle. We must set the level of our communication to the audience. If our message is too complex for them they will stop listening with their minds, although they appear to be awake!

UNCLEAR This does not necessarily mean a mumbled or garbled message; that would be easy to spot. By unclear, we also mean a bad logical composition. It's essential to get a message across to someone in such a way that the listener almost leads himself to the answer by the power of the logic in the message.

JARGON There is plenty of this about today, and we hope we haven't fallen into the trap by using it somewhere in this book! Jargon is, of course, special language that all industries have appropriate to their industry. In computer language, for example, there is hardware, software, interface and many others. Don't use much jargon when reporting upwards unless you're quite sure your receiver understands.

FEAR A lot more people than one might realise don't communicate on certain issues because they are fearful of the consequences. They are worried about whether they will look foolish or even worse.

There are many more one might list and it is certainly useful to examine oneself and the environment in which one works to find obstacles to communication which one can help to remove. A company problem, as distinct from individual, is sometimes the complete lack of a communications policy. There should be one in every company where it is no longer possible for the owner or general manager to talk to everyone at fairly regular intervals. If a policy does not exist then a vacuum forms as far as information is concerned. Such situations breed rumours and non-facts faster than any other. If you are in the position to do so try to ensure that a communications policy exists. This will consist of company instructions, company announcements, department information, suggestion schemes and the like. Probably more important, however, is for your staff to feel *you* keep them informed. There will sometimes be things you cannot tell them, but they want to be kept 'in the picture' and should be as much as you possibly can.

This feeling of 'belonging' is not just a 'good' thing to do for human relations. It can help any company or organisation to achieve better results if people get a greater awareness of what is going on. The problem of communication in, say, a large government department is immense. There may be anything from 20 to 100,000 people. Furthermore a department may be scattered over London in perhaps 30 or 40 buildings and indeed in offices anywhere in the United Kingdom. However, without good communication there are many interplays that will not take place and we get the old problem of the left hand not knowing what the right is doing in the public eye.

This means it is essential to spend money on communication, probably with a senior official in charge of it, and to supplement this by news-sheets, information circulars and the like. However, once again the communication foundations will depend upon the way the top managers communicate with one another, and likewise with the subordinates.

Unfortunately, it is also a fact that up to 60 per cent or more of information that ought to be transferred is lost in the filter action of management chains in most large departments and industries.

Staff Communications

In talking with our staff there are generally five things we shall be dealing with:

Telling them to do something.
Telling them about something.
Listening to their personal or work problems, and this includes asking questions.
Guiding them in some way.
Discussing common problems.

In all of these it is necessary for the manager to make as much contribution to successful communication as he can and that will include some time to study the situations. Knowledge of background and personalities helps considerably the 'listening' part of the communications. The sort of remark that can ruin a discussion is to say to a rather hot tempered person: 'You know the trouble with you George is. . . .' Immediately the receiver of such a statement is on guard, and easy communication may either not be possible or take a long time to restore.

In telling your staff to do something it should be done in such a way that the reason for telling, even if the facts are unpleasant, are understood. Most people, basically, want to understand, but there are so many communication difficulties about that it may seem sometimes as though they don't.

In communicating with your staff you will always get more response by leading them to a conclusion rather than by simply telling them. They have got to understand, to agree the conclusion is the right one and then say to themselves: I've got this message clear. I may not care for the content but it is right.

In listening to their work problems bear in mind that good listening is important to both of you if the job is to proceed in the best manner. How can you instruct, help or guide a man with a problem if you don't understand the problem properly?

If the problem is personal, then of course sympathetic listening is very important, but any advice you may give must clearly be shown to be your personal opinion not your company's, unless the two are really interwoven, in which case your competence to deal with it must be clear. Certainly items like purchasing a house or investing can be answered with frankness, but the answer is your opinion, not your guarantee.

Communicating with Your Manager

First of all, we hope he listens. It can be maddening when the 'boss' never listens. If you find this is so there may be something you can do about it. Analyse the problem. Is it because he is just that sort of person and in fact he doesn't listen to anybody? Is it because you are so uninteresting or long winded or both he dare not take a chance on listening to you?

A manager wants information in the fastest time provided it is factual and meaningful. There is so much potential information hanging over his head that if it all fell on him he would not have time to do his job. Keep it short, is a good moral.

KEYS TO SUCCESS

These are the keys to successful communication with your manager. Be:

Timely.	Factual.
Short.	Unambiguous.
Meaningful.	Convincing.

Timeliness is obviously important. Old information on current problems is usually useless and if quick decisions have to be made the manager also wants the relevant information quickly. There will be little thanks for out-of-date information.

If the message is short the manager is almost bound to read it. If it is long he may put it aside, only skim it, give it to somebody else to read or find it difficult to get the facts because they are surrounded by irrelevancy. The manager's time is precious. A long message is also most prone to mistakes and wandering off the point. It is worth the effort to get the message short.

Even though short, your information must still be meaningful. Half a message that doesn't answer the question is still useless. The manager then may have to ask again (or ignore you next time) and this takes up more valuable time. The receiver as he reads your message should get a clear picture of what you wanted to say.

If what you have to say is not factual then unless you are very clear about this point and explain the basis of your hypothesis your manager will wonder what reliance he may place in you. He will respect facts and the intelligent use of theories stated to be such. Many situations are not so easy as to be quickly and conveniently expressed as fact. Judgement must be included. It should be clearly labelled as such. Although most people start off in the belief that the message is true, disbelief and, far worse, disenchantment of the sender will follow quickly.

Ambiguity is a subtle enemy. You write what you think is an excellent, clear message and what does the silly chap who receives it do? He says he cannot understand it: it might mean this or might mean that. Before you argue with him, be careful. Unless he is deliberately trying to be awkward *he* probably genuinely does see more than one interpretation and after all he is reading it. We must watch ambiguity carefully and try and put ourselves in the reader's place. What possible misconstruction could there be?

The last of our keys to success in communicating with our manager is convincing him our solution or recommendation is the right one. We hope we are much more than halfway because we have been careful so far. Now we need the extra push, the final argument to clinch the matter. This is worth some thought as the whole object of communication is to get the desired effect from the message.

WHAT DOES HE WANT TO HEAR?

We've already said that all managers want to spend their time wisely. With this in mind what does your manager want to hear? He certainly doesn't want a running commentary on your work or even all your achievements listed. What he does want to hear are reports from you on anticipated divergencies of budget, time plans or performance of your agreed work objectives. He will want to know whether these are temporary setbacks and for how long, or whether the original plan is likely to permanently suffer. He will also want to hear of major achievements in the performance of the work as these add credence to both your efforts and his towards the total goals.

The general rules for effective communication we have already listed, but it is worth trying to submit your information in a way that the manager understands best. This may be in simple written form, or charts or diagram. All managers have their own pet preferences. If you can find your manager's preferred method it will probably save you a lot of time in the future. It takes time to communicate and the sender must help the receiver in order to get the desired response.

twelve Does Organisation Matter?

Introduction

What is an organisation? To many people, especially in the larger company there is an awareness of organisation ranging from acute in the case of 'our' department to a rather hazy idea of the existence of other departments. The problem is, of course, that each of us fits at the same time into little private worlds of our own with wife, husband or family, immediate company colleagues and others outside the working environment. These may include the sports or social club where some organisation is necessary. They must have committees and officers to run them otherwise it would not be possible to raise money to run the club or to get teams and equipment together.

In all these our purpose, generally, is to play some useful part, to live enjoyably and work to some advantage. The company, however, exists basically to make money for the proprietors whether these are private owners or shareholders in a public company. Even in nationalised industries the aim is to make a profit. We know there are many other motives which raise a company above the level of a mere profit making machine, but whatever is said on the subject there is little doubt that the profit motive in one form or another is the main aim. Now join the company and its motives with the ideals of the men or women working for it. What must the company do to maximise their effort and also satisfy their wants? In other words how can the company organise its work force to be most effective? We say *organise*. This means to give an orderly structure to, to put into working order or to make arrangements

96

for, as the Concise Oxford Dictionary describes it. In a small one-man company the total organisation is the proprietor. He is production worker, manager, accountant and inventor. There is no personnel problem, only himself. If he is effective he rewards himself. In a larger company there must obviously be some way in which the many functions are knitted together to promote the most effective end result.

This then is the framework in which we work. It will provide a system of authority and responsibility as well as one for the flow of information and instructions. It enables a division of duties to be defined.

Working organisations are of the utmost importance to managers. A clerk, engineer, programmer or production worker can do a day's work without knowing anything more about the organisation in which he works than the name of his boss. For a manager to make a really effective contribution to the aims of his company, he must know how it is organised. Not only does he need to know the organisation, even more important he must understand it.

Forms of Organisation

The traditional forms of organisation are authoritarian and hierarchical. Military organisation is typical of the traditional style. One man commands a unit and there is a direct chain of command through a pyramid of sub-unit commanders down to the private soldiers. There is no ambiguity about it. Every man in the organisation has one boss and one only. Orders flow quickly and smoothly down through the chain of command.

Most business organisations are based on the principles of the traditional or hierarchical organisation. These are:

1 Each man or woman looks to only one person for his instructions.
2 The number of people whom any one manager can effectively control is limited. For a mixed team with each man handling a different kind of work, the limit is probably five or six. Where the subordinates are doing identical work the span of control can go up to thirty or more.
3 Chains of command are kept as short as possible. Long chains of command lead to distortion of information flows.

Such an organisation is ideal for the fairly rigid control of a firm. It is, however, fairly inflexible and cannot react swiftly to change.

The traditional division of labour in industry is:

H

97

Engineering.
Manufacturing.
Marketing.
Accounts and Administration.

As companies become larger so they are divided into smaller and smaller specialities.

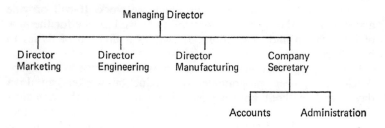

Fig.1

Company organisations are generally promulgated in the form of organisation charts. A simple one might be as shown in Figure 1. One of the disadvantages of this form of chart is that one man appears to be above another, to be a superior person. Of course none, or very few people, think of themselves as being 'below'. One managing director tried to get around this by drawing his organisational charts in the form of Figure 2. Instructions, or commands, flowed from left to right. No significance was attached to vertical positions which as far as possible were arranged in alphabetic order.

It is unfortunately necessary, at least in companies of any size, to publish organisation charts. Unless we publish them there is danger of confusion. Even if each manager knows what he himself is

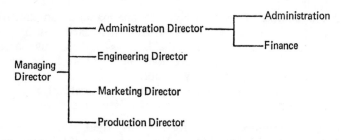

Fig.2

98

responsible for, there is a danger of overlap and also of gaps between the boundaries of individual authority. A good organisation chart helps to highlight such gaps and overlaps and hence, hopefully, leads to action to overcome them. We say unfortunately because the mere publication of organisation charts leads to a degree of ossification in an organisation. The organisation is enshrined in the chart and no responsibility can change until it has been duly promulgated as an amendment to the chart. Needless to say any reasonably flexible company publishes its charts in loose-leaf form to allow for frequent amendment.

Fixed organisations of this sort also tend to put blinkers on people. Middle and junior managers sometimes lose sight of the real aims of their company in their concentration on their own speciality. To overcome the problems of rigidity and reduction in individual responsibility two trends are discernible.

First there is an attempt to break down large organisations into smaller self-accounting, self-driving units, which are complete in themselves. The units specialise in one aspect of a company's business. They have all the functions, marketing, production, etc, which they need to operate. They have their own general manager or managing director who has responsibility for running them with minimum guidance from the parent company and from his own board. His board is probably made up of executives from the parent company. Similarly devolution of authority may be sought in a retail chain by giving a great deal of responsibility to individual store managers.

The second trend is the attempt to move away from authoritarian organisations to very flexible organisation where roles change as the requirements of the situation demand.

The one thing we can be sure about it is that the perfect organisation has not yet been evolved and furthermore probably never will. Organisations have to be evolved to meet the particular needs of a particular company (or nationalised industry). There can be no universal solution. The demands on a commercial bank with hundreds of branches are very different to those on a specialised merchant bank. Both again are different to the demands on an engineering based manufacturing company or a software house.

Additionally, company organisation has to change to meet the continuing change in the external environment. The impact of external influences—shareholders, customers, suppliers, trade unions, recruitment sources, local and central government—must be reflected in the company organisation.

Setting up an Organisation

In setting up any organisation there are several guiding principles we should follow. Firstly, we must ask ourselves: What are the objectives of the organisation? What are we trying to achieve? Only the realities of the situation should be taken in account, the most sensible assumptions. These questions will reveal the broad answer: that, say, we need a large marketing division; a small engineering and production division because we intend to 'buy in' the bulk of our products; an advanced quality assurance and checking division to check our products; a large maintenance on all products; a large maintenance division because we intend to offer maintenance on all products—and so on until a picture emerges of the general organisation pattern. In carrying out such a survey it must be assumed that the answers are justified in economic terms, for example that it is possible and planned to bring a correct share of profit into the company from maintenance activities and/or that the quality assurance activity can pay for itself over the range of products.

Having painted the broad picture, we must next examine the likely changes that could and then must occur quickly and without upheaval in the event that either the plan does not make good in one area or another or that expansion is more rapid. Will the organisation be able to adapt quickly to change?

If the answer to this is satisfactory, then the organisation balance will begin to emerge and the question of one large unit or separate smaller units must arise. Both arrangements are successfully practised; in the one case with strong control on all aspects of the business from the centre, in the other, separate accounting units with autonomy and a minimum of central control. Companies that operate in the second manner have in general two different methods of allowing freedom. It can be very free in that the manager or director of one of the units not only has all of the marketing and other functions completely under his charge, but that he also raises his own finance and in that sense is very independent. His 'accounting' is his effectiveness overall to the central holding company. In the other method everything is similar except the provision of finance, which has to be obtained from the parent company. In both cases profitability and accounting ratios to check overall effectiveness are the controlling influences.

Whether we now discuss the one large unit or one of the smaller accounting units there are further structural points that can make or mar the organisation.

Leadership must start at the top. Democracy, freedom and incentive all have their place, but no company can exist for long without control from the top. Whether this control is the delicate probing of a fine lance at all the tender spots of a company such that control seems minimal or whether it is more urgent and heavy, control there must be.

If we have a large number of management levels there are three dangers:

1 Communications from the top, including decisions that in any company sometimes must be made at the top, will be bad. There will be a failure to seize opportunities or react quickly enough to new situations. The information to make decisions will be late or non-existent.

2 Co-ordination of tasks that affect more than one department will be poor. There is a high probability of waste through more meetings, committees, working parties, etc. Projects will be difficult to complete. Because of the real danger of overlapping authority and low task yield, management will grow fat and lazy. A self-perpetuating bureaucracy will grow up with detailed built in procedures.

3 Management performance will not grow but will fall. While, due to the many levels, there may appear to be more chances of promotion for those managers who want challenge will find none. There will be many examples of managers badly under-employed with consequent job dissatisfaction and frustration. The younger or better managers will migrate to better jobs.

This means severe dangers of the business falling away or being held back by a shortage of good men.

What now of the opposite case, that of too few managers with very wide responsibilities. There will be plenty of challenge, nobody will have time to grow fat and lazy and the organisation will hum with activity for a while. Performance will gradually fall as managers become less effective due to overload or, in the worse case, disappear six feet under! Staff under the manager will find he is always too busy to see them and job outlines will be poor. This arrangement is no better in the end than the first.

A minimum number of management levels must be arranged, the responsibilities as wide as such as possible but job objectives carefully agreed and calculated such that they are possible, but hard enough to make the manager grow in his task. He has, however, a proper chance of retaining his health, his wisdom and his enthusiasm. All these are essential for the company as well. The exact structure can only be worked out in a particular situation, but the dangers above can be realised and taken into account. By looking around at other companies it becomes clear that their organisation and way of working varies. We favour the decentralised company, a great freedom in the small unit so formed with a central headquarters unit able to ensure the essential standards of profitability and effectiveness. This may be done by the central unit asking the right questions and being able to give the right guidance and advice if required. The general lessons of history and industry need to be learnt, by all of us. In history the big empires perish, in industry they often get less effective and might perish unless they frequently up-date their organisations. In industry the young small companies have an enthusiasm that the larger ones often lack, while the larger ones seem always to promise economies of size and never quite make it.

You may say 'But I'm not likely to be in such a position to set up a large organisation, where is the advice for me?' The comment seems fair at first sight, but as one goes through the steps in setting up an organisation one eventually realises that the steps are common for both large and small organisations. Whatever organisation you are called on to start or change the lessons hold good:

Plan the objectives of the organisation with realism.
Look at the tolerances of the objectives.
Decide on the broad principles of the organisation.
Decide the sub-objectives and the spans of control.
Objectives must be hard enough to keep a manager growing in his abilities but be attainable and realistic.

Make sure that the organisation you fashion is able to communicate quickly and effectively within itself. This is a good test for the right sort of organisation. Finally an organisation must be dynamic, flexible, able to adjust itself to change. If it becomes an impediment and out of touch then sort it out before it becomes an organisation to sustain itself and not the business.

Our Own Actions

Most of us in fact work in companies which are fairly rigidly organised. We have to recognise that life is not rigid and inflexible and that in practice people adapt to a rigid organisational structure.

102

In the process they modify the working of the organisation and an informal organisation grows up within the formal one. The informal organisation reflects realities. It takes account of which sleepy managers should be bypassed. It recognises that some managers and some departments abdicate their responsibilities. The boundaries laid out so rigidly in theory can be crossed.

One barrier to communication across organisational boundaries is suspicion and mistrust. You should try to overcome this as far as your own department or section is concerned. One way of doing it is to try to attach your people for periods of a few days or weeks to the departments they have to deal with. It makes it a lot easier for them to get things done if they have met, and worked, eaten and drunk with the people concerned. It also pays to welcome people from other parts of the company on attachment or even day visits to your section. Where your work is very dependent on the work of another department in the company regular two-way visits and attachments should be fostered. If your company has an active sports life encourage your people to develop their contacts in the club.

Of course, you yourself must spend an appreciable amount of time developing contacts across the company's organisational boundaries. Go out of your way to visit other parts of the company. Welcome visitors yourself and make a point of making them feel welcome. If they come unannounced, find time to talk to them and give them a cup of tea or coffee. If they come at the appropriate time go out to lunch with them. If other parts of the company ask for your help, give it, even if it causes you considerable inconvenience. Invitations from the sales force to talk to their customers or prospective customers should be accepted wherever possible. Be prepared at any time to lecture about your work and the work of your section. It probably pays to have preprepared sets of lecture notes to enable you to give talks of varying lengths to varying audiences.

As well as recognising the informal links which can be built up to smooth your work in an organisation we must also recognise the fact that conflict exists within organisations. There may well be a conflict of interest between managers. In large companies many managers' interests may legitimately be in conflict. Superimposed on this is the conflict arising from personal ambitions and jealousies. No manager should be surprised at the existence of these conflicts. If he is prepared for them he can help to resolve them. A golden rule to remember is that so long as you win the war you can afford to lose some of the battles.

"CONGRATULATIONS, MISS JONES—YOUR LONG TERM PROJECTIONS ARE WELL IN FRONT"

part three Managing Money

thirteen Your Own First

As an introduction to the next few chapters, and to give an impetus to the closer examination of your investments and savings, etc, we devote this short chapter. It is only an introduction, a reminder how to do a few of the calculations used in savings and purchases involving interest. Taxation effects are deliberately omitted as the rates and the law applicable to reliefs can vary. We have already mentioned in Chapter 4 the desirability of independence through savings or good financial practice. What follows may help to achieve this.

House Purchase

It is useful, perhaps one might think essential, to be able to check the figures involved as probably it is the largest purchase most of us make in our lives. There is a family of formulæ involved in all these calculations involving interest, and for a reducing debt type of loan with interest charged on the remainder as with a building society the formulæ is:

$$P/R = \frac{(1+I)^n - 1}{I(1+I)^n}$$

Where P is the capital sum or loan initially borrowed, R the annual payment, I the interest per cent and n the term of years. The assumption in this formula is that payments are made yearly in arrears and that interest is charged on the first day of each year.

Taking, say, a 20 year mortgage at $8\frac{1}{2}$ per cent on £10,000 borrowed, what can we find out about it? Substituting the 20 years and the $8\frac{1}{2}$ per cent in the formula we have:

$$P/R = \frac{(1+0.085)^{20}-1}{0.085\,(1+0.085)^{20}} = 9.46 \text{ (approx.)}$$

Thus for £10,000 the yearly amount to pay is $10,000/9.46 =$ £1,057.

Comparing this with some building society tables shows small differences in the region of £1 between some of them.

The advantage of getting the figure of 9.46 is that if we can fix the term of years and the interest, which is usually fixed for us anyway, we can then rapidly compare amounts against yearly payments. If you can find some tables laid out in a convenient manner then you don't need to work the sums out but usually once you've got the 9.46 figure or its equivalent for a different number of years, it is simpler to work out a spot case than it is to find some tables with the right quotation.

What now of the case where we have paid off several years' mortgage payments and want to know how much we now owe? Let us say 5 years' payments have been made. We use this time the formula

$$d = \frac{R+(PI-R)\,(1+I)^{n_1}}{I}$$

where d is the balance of debt, P the original debt, R and I as in previous example and n_1 the years paid so far. In this example, therefore, we have:

$$d = \frac{1{,}057+\left[\dfrac{(10{\cdot}000 \times 0{\cdot}085)-1{,}057}{0{\cdot}085}\right](1{\cdot}085)^5}{ }$$

$$= \frac{1{,}057+(850-1{,}057)\,(1{\cdot}085)^5}{0{\cdot}085}$$

$$= \frac{1{,}057-(207 \times 1{\cdot}5)}{0{\cdot}085} = \text{£8,782}$$

So after 5 years' payments we owe £8,782 out of our original £10,000 borrowed. This is of course the general problem in borrowing in that in the early years the yearly payback consists mostly of interest. In the example quoted in the first year we will pay back £1,057−850 = £207.

In fact a closer examination of the first 5 years is interesting.

	1 Total interest	2 Interest reduction per year	3 Total payback
	£	£	£	£
Initial debt	10,000			
Interest 1st year	850	850	—	—
	10,850			
Payback 1st year	1,057	—	—	1,057
	9,793			
Interest 2nd year	833	833	17	—
	10,626			
Payback 2nd year	1,057	—	—	1,057
	9,569			
Interest 3rd year	823	823	27	—
	10,392			
Payback 3rd year	1,057	—	—	1,057
	9,335			
Interest 4th year	793	793	57	—
	10,128			
Payback 4th year	1,057	—	—	1,057
	9,071			
Interest 5th year	771	771	79	—
	9,842			
Payback 5th year	1,057	—	—	1,057
Balance at end of 5th year	8,785	4,070	—	5,285

The progress towards total paying off is of course slow, but the interest reduction is gathering momentum as evidenced by column 2. It is clear from the figures that although house value appreciation is one of the best hedges against inflation, there are expenses involved.

The taxation relief on house mortgage will not confuse the figures so far. The effect of the tax relief is to put extra money back into the pay packet each month, i.e. less tax to pay (providing that income tax is paid). Usually the tax relief, plus the fact that the mortgage interest could be considered as equivalent to rental means that buying one's own house is a very worthwhile investment. Most of us prefer a roof rather than a tent and a house can be sold and another bought, the appreciation on the first keeping up with increased price of the next one.

Savings

If we want to save money over a number of years at an interest rate (I) we can calculate the final sum for regular payments from

$$A = R\left[\frac{(1+I)^n - 1}{I}\right]$$

where A is the amount to be saved, R the regular amount saved per year and I the interest per cent. This is called a sinking fund calculation and there are tables available which make the calculations much simpler, for example those by Lawson and Windle published by Oliver & Boyd, Edinburgh.

If we save £500 per year at 8 per cent interest how much shall we have in 15 years? From tables we can get the value of

$$\frac{(1+I)^n - 1}{I}$$

so that the only arithmetic we shall have to do is $A = R(x)$ where $(x) =$ table value of

$$\frac{(1+I)^n - 1}{I}$$

In this example the (x) is 27·152, so $A = 500 \times 27·152 = £13,576·00$. As we can see the amount saved without interest is only $500 \times 15 = £7,500$ so that the interest over the term has doubled the total net savings.

This assumes the savings are put in over each year, but interest is only paid on what is there at the end of the year. Since this will be paid a year later there is in effect 14 lots of interest for 15 lots of savings since we assume we draw the money out at the end of 15 years. Once again the real build up of interest, like the capital in the house purchase scheme, occurs in the later years. If you laid out the complete set of figures you would find for instance that in the eighth year the yearly interest is £357 whereas in the fifteenth year it is £968.

By using tables the sums become so easy that we can start to compare one sort of savings against another quite easily and to our long-term benefit. Some will, of course, be affected by taxation rules at the time, but these effects can be taken into account. The main advantage is to get us thinking about and comparing one sort of savings with another.

Another way of looking at the savings problem is to say 'What sum of money must I save every year for 10 years to give me a capital sum then of, say, £28,000 assuming I can expect a tax free interest rate of 5 per cent?' This time we have the formula

$$R = A \; \frac{I}{(1+I)^n - 1}$$

As we can see the real 'formula' part is the reciprocal of the previous example. Another set of tables giving the values for

$$\frac{I}{(1+I)^n - 1}$$

shows that for 10 years and 5 per cent the figure is 0·07950. Therefore:

$$R = £28,000 \times 0·07950$$

$$= £2,226$$

fourteen Budgets and Measurements of Performance

Introduction

All business involves the management of money. You remember Charles Dickens' character Micawber who found happiness in spending 6d less than his weekly income and misery when he spent 6d more. The same thing applies to business as to private individuals and business must strive to maximise its profit. In business especially we have to plan for such profit and we do it by budgeting. This is in essence writing down a simple sum that says:

Money coming in	£10,000,000
Money going out	£8,000,000
Profit (before taxation)	£2,000,000

Is it only money we are budgeting? Money certainly is the measure, but what we are really doing is planning resources and that means human beings as well. Throughout this book we have emphasised the human aspects, and when talking about money, balance sheets, cash flow and the like we always have to consider the two great human aspects of all business:

The contribution from people in physical and mental effort.
The effects of the business upon people inside or outside the business.

In preparing a budget we could be preparing a budget for sales, i.e. money coming in or a budget for manufacture, i.e. money going out. In the most simple terms the difference between the two is the profit of the company.

The sales budget, however, will be twofold. Firstly, the contribution from salesmen will be assessed in terms of sales targets by area, region, country or type, etc, to comprise a total sales revenue budget. Secondly, the cost budget of the salesmen's salaries and overheads will be prepared. There will be constant adjustments to get the maximum return from sales for the minimum effort, but taking into account strategic issues as well as tactical. For example, it may be worth spending money for a certain sales area or activity although the likely sales may take much longer to effect. Competition may be heavy in some areas, not in others. Is it worth heavily spending in highly competitive areas rather than consolidating less competitive ones? This sort of question affects people all the time: salesmen's jobs, personnel training, administration and many others. The result in money terms will look much colder and less exciting, as though people had never been invented, for example:

		Sales revenue	Sales expenditure
Area	A	£3·4m	£85·5K
	B	£2·7m	£60·0K
	C	£1·8m	£42·3K
Totals		£7·9m	£187·8K

How does all this Budgeting start in a Company?

The board of directors will have before them three basic items of information which will have taken a great deal of preparation before summarisation was possible. Much of this information must come from estimates passed up and adjusted, step by step, up the management tree. It may be in fairly rough form at this stage, but does reflect the likely required expenditure. The three items are:

1 Previous budgets and targets with the actual outcome.
2 Market potential.
3 Resource potential including cash position.

Past history if available provides experience for future judgement. It is not infallible advice either for 'We did it once we can do it again' or 'We have never done anything like it before.'

The market potential requires specialist investigation into all the possible areas, probably test marketing in some trades, certainly much study of trends and fashions in all types of business. Knowledge of what probable competitors are doing or are likely to do is highly desirable.

The resource potential is only elastic to a degree. It will take time to increase a labour force, time to develop new products and time to sell them. Equally difficult is the arrangement to get an adequate cash flow to underwrite an increase in effort. Money will be needed to sustain development of a product, to pay for engineers and salesmen; the revenue from sales may be a year or more later than the major expenditures of development and manufacture. How much cash can be put at risk and paid back, let alone obtained at all is a matter of the deepest concern for the principals of the business.

A decision will eventually be taken. The business will spend £x on development, £y on sales and overheads, £z on manufacture. The income from sales will be £A. Profit $= A - (x + y + z)$. This is the stem of all the budgets. A complete breakdown can not be made in all the departments of the business until the detailed budgets adjusted by management discussion when added together equal the above summary.

How far ahead can a Company Budget?

We ought to take several views of the road ahead in a company. We ought to take a long look, 3–5 years or even longer. Even at 3 years the view will not be all that clear in many companies and at 5 years somewhat misty! However, there is little doubt we should attempt to look that far, to set our sights. It is quite a bit like a ship's journey. If there is no place to aim for, the journey will become a meandering over the oceans. If there is a final goal then all the intermediate planning, navigation, etc, is towards that goal. In business it helps the 1 and 2 year budgeting if there is a longer-term plan existing. Plans will change of course. No management however astute and skilled can control external or even all internal circumstances, but what they can do is to have alternative plans available to deal with such situations. The right course is therefore:

1 To set a long-term plan.
2 To set short- and medium-term plans within the framework of (1).
3 To be ready for change.

114

What can Your Important Contribution be to Budgeting?

The most important one will be not to accept what has gone before as a sacred criterion for the future. Your responsibility must always be to arrange your budget so that you get more results for less cost. Easy to say, not always to do, but new ways of achieving goals have to be continuously explored. A good start for example is not to assume automatically that any merit rises for staff are going to increase the staff budget. Why not look into the quality of the staff instead. It is often a fact that fewer, better paid, higher quality staff will do the same if not more work than lower paid, lesser quality staff. This is especially true in high technology areas such as computer programming or design engineering. Additionally, it may be possible to substitute business machinery for men so that the discounted capital is less expensive than the previous staff payroll.

Productivity gains in two ways from a new, hard look at the value for money position in terms of staffing. Firstly, less total wages for the same output or more relative output means more profit. Secondly, encouragement for those who deserve it is likely to make them work better and others to strive a bit harder to obtain it.

Surely this is fairer to the majority even if a small number have to suffer temporarily. There may be other ways that would work. For instance, if some departments are over-manned and others under-manned then training may be the answer to fill vacancies and cream off surpluses. Natural wastage may take care of part of the problem.

Business machinery leading to automation; dreadful words these in some ears, but man's ingenuity will not cease and more and more automation must come. The budget is affected in three ways. The cost of capital to buy machinery must be added to the budget; some people will be unwanted and their pay is saved; new people will probably be required to operate or mind the new machines. Will all this reduce the budget? It may do or it may allow increased sales for the same cost because the individual product cost can be reduced because a larger quantity is produced. Appropriate management has to assess the effects and budgets will have to be looked at again in many areas of the business.

What we have said so far should show clearly that budgets are not the inanimate toys of accountants but the living being of the business. They affect humans greatly and humans can effect much by them. You can, therefore, play a significant part in your company, great or small, by using any budget you may control as an instrument of innovation and change to obtain better productivity, profitability and above all value for money.

Budgets in Practice

We have discussed the philosophy of the budget, the human scene behind the budget, but what of the mechanics of budgeting, the task you will do? The budget may be large or small, the accounting system good or indifferent. From top management must come initially a budget framework. Suppose that in a moderately sized manufacturing company there are directorates for:

Engineering and manufacturing	(£5m)
Marketing	(£2m)
Finance and administration	(£1m)
Personnel and training	(£1m)
	£9m

and that after discussion the board may decide that the operating expenditure for the year will be as marked in £m.

This will have been done in relation to the planned turnover and profit, and management lower down will have assisted in the preparation for their respective directorates. The total cash flow position may then look something like this:

Turnover £15m	
Operating expenditure	£9m
Funding costs	£1m
Profit before tax	£5m
	£15m

This is the grand plan thrashed out at board level from the three principals we mentioned earlier including overall cash flow.

From this the individual directors can now start going down the management tree distributing budget allocations in accordance with the total at their disposal. It may be that the original budgets requested by the operating managers can be met or some may have to be adjusted up or down. With the budgets will come firm agreed objectives, e.g. sales manager district A will have target sales of £2m for his portion of the operating budget.

DETAILING A BUDGET

Going back to the first phase of budget preparation the board of the company has to obtain estimates of the total operating expenditure based upon a particular corporate policy. In detail this may represent, say, an engineering manager having to estimate for the design and development cost of a new product, a manufacturing manager for the production engineering and manufacture of the product and the sales organisation for selling it. It should be noted that these estimates may be the whole or only a part of the activities of the management concerned. The total budget formation is on a 'tree' basis as shown in Figure 3. The detailed budget itself will be made up basically from the cost of labour, materials and overheads.

A particular company will have its own method of gathering these costs together. An example is here given of Company ABC showing the many types of items that could comprise a budget. There would also be other backing information necessary, e.g. salaries would stem from different grades and skills of individuals

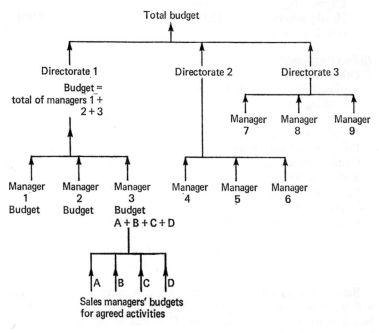

Fig.3

117

so that apart from money, if the company wished to know the numbers of logic designers, draughtsmen, project engineers, etc, it could cross total these from the appropriate budgets.

Company ABC
PROJECT ENGINEERING DIVISION

Budget for Year 19 /19 (Year 1)			Projected expenditure Year 19 /19 (Year 2)
	£	£	£
Direct expenditure			
Project salaries		40,000	45,000
Materials and subcontracts			
Purchases	50,000		
Subcontracts	20,000	70,000	60,000
Inter Division			
Engineering	10,000		
Headquarters	15,000	25,000	17,000
(Rent and overheads) ———			
Indirect expenditure			
Other salaries		6,000	
National Insurance and pensions		2,300	
Travelling expenses		3,000	
Entertainment		300	
Repairs and maintenance		400	
Printing and stationery		1,000	23,000
General expenses		2,000	
Staff training		700	
Publications and books		50	
Depreciation		300	
Charges from other areas		10,000	
TOTAL		£161,050	£145,000

Before you as an effective manager can prepare a budget you will want to know and agree with your management at least the broad outline of your objectives. This will enable you to decide how you will achieve those objectives and what resources are required. Although money is the end result the value is built up from this knowledge of resource requirements. You must fit your own type of business details to your budget, but if you systematically go through the resource list and then apply some value for money techniques, such as mentioned later, you are likely to produce an effective budget.

Firstly the task(s), whatever it is, will require labour, male and/ or female, over the entire timescale. It may build up to a peak, particularly in the case of one off projects or it may be a steady quantity, thus dictating to some extent the amount of work you can do. This is where some innovation may pay dividends.

You may be able to effectively increase your manpower effort by business machinery or more efficient working arrangements. You have to work on such ideas. How many men to do a job will be largely a question of past performance plus future promise and ideas for improvement. Your type of industry averages should be known to you. If the task is brand new and there are no criterion then as a manager you have to use your skills, experience, common sense and entrepreneurial thinking to make a decision on the basis of estimation. That's what at least half your salary should be for. You must also shop around for ideas. You finally produce a manpower plan or a plan of work you can do with a fixed labour force. Next come all the extras to human involvement: National Insurance pensions, expenses of all types, consumable items like pencils and paper and training allowances. Study existing budgets in your company and elsewhere to make yourself out a comprehensive list. Usually a lot of the 'overheads' to salaries are a fixed proportion or can often be treated as such. Your own company may in fact do it that way and avoid some of the separate entries.

Secondly, there are charges levied by either the company headquarters or other departments for such items as equipment depreciation or rent for the premises you occupy, and various services to be supplied during the year, e.g. drawing, designing or manufacturing something for you. Thirdly, your budget may involve outside purchases of general goods and equipment, parts or assemblies or additional manpower. Any of the above will break down into further categories to help build up the whole.

REJECTION

What unfortunately often happens is that a budget is prepared with the best intention and is rejected with the curt comment, 'Reduce by 10 per cent!' There can be two main reasons for this.

One is that the company would overtrade without such a cut and the other is that your management believes you are just too high by some amount, not necessarily exactly 10 per cent. What do you do about it?

The first action is not to get all upset about the so-and-so management above. Just think for a moment about the chap above your own manager who, even when he gets his first look at the budgets from his five or six managers finds that the total is one and a half times what he expects his total budget will be! You have only your own to worry about; he has to suffer the inflation of budgets from perhaps 25 departments.

Now go through every figure again in your budget. If you had to guess a bit before in one area or another take a much closer look, try to substantiate the figures. Have you put some contingency in that has no real justification?

Examine every item again with a view to reducing it by 15 to 20 per cent and see what it would do. If in the end you've managed to cut your budget estimate by 5 per cent and any further cuts would affect staffing or the amount of work you really believe your department can do then go back to your manager and say so. Be sure of your facts! You may find that this is accepted, that the 10 per cent was an aim and that 5 per cent will be all right. If more savings are required the management above will either order a general cut for all, or start to selectively axe one or more budgets. If the order is cuts all round, then you have to do it and this may mean staff cuts, of course. Budgets are live things, they are always a battle of compromise between what we'd like and what we can get.

Inflation

This process seems to stay with us whatever new economic theories are tried out. In budgeting, of course, it is an ever present challenge. It is only too easy to set next year's budget 7 per cent up on this one for inflation reasons alone. The result must be either a 7 per cent fall in profits or a rise in prices to fully or partly compensate. The challenge is to find ways of cutting costs to help combat this creeping evil. With large staffs the inflation of wages problem is acute. There is no easy solution; the answer lies in hard work and thought, technical and management innovation, and a knowledge of the need for an answer to be found.

fifteen Understanding the Company's Money

The Balance Sheet

What do the words 'balance sheet' mean to you? Accountants' jargon? Something you don't have to worry about? Something you need not understand? Let us reserve judgement until we have looked much more closely into just what a balance sheet is. It's a still picture of a company's financial state at one particular moment of time. Pay one more salary, buy one more desk or pay an electricity bill and a new balance sheet is required. For this reason it seems impracticable to prepare a balance sheet too often and most companies do it once a year. This is not to say that the information in the balance sheet is not required much more often. In fact with computer based management information systems it would be perfectly feasible to display the major aspects of the balance sheet of a company on a display screen and have it brought up to date, say, every hour or so. In those companies today which have a sophisticated management accounting system, daily balances are provided to top management. In a great many companies, unfortunately, the information is far less frequently prepared.

WHAT A BALANCE SHEET LOOKS LIKE

Most of us have seen balance sheets. They come in many different forms but they all show the same information, i.e. a list of assets on the right-hand side of the sheet and a list of liabilities on the left. It is a statement of outstanding balances in the books of the company after a profit and loss account preparation. The assets total must equal the liabilities total after the insertion of a net loss or

121

net profit into the balance sheet. A very simple example would be the ownership of a house. We own a house to live in, but also to hope it will be some hedge against inflation. We hope it will always reflect 'present day' values.

Liabilities		Assets	
Building society	£5,000	House valued at	£10,000
Original capital put into house	£2,000		
Capital payments to building society	£1,000	Representing total	
Appreciation since purchase (profit)	£2,000	'capital'	
	£10,000		£10,000

It may seem wrong to show the capital we invested and the appreciation since purchase as 'liabilities'. This arises from the fact that the total assets must have an equal 'claim' against them as far as the balance sheet is concerned. These 'liabilities' as they are called are, in this case, partly comprised of external liability to the building society and partly our own capital.

Assets—External liabilities = Capital

The real asset in this case is the house, the real liability is the amount owed to the building society.

The total capital, in the form of original and paid capital and the appreciation, must therefore be put on the liabilities' side to balance against the assets. In all cases the capital of a business, or as in the example above, will be found on the liability side of the balance sheet. It should be noted that in, say, a year's time if a further balance sheet was struck the amount owed to the building society would be less, the appreciation more and thus the total capital increased by these two changes. For example:

Liabilities		Assets	
Building society	£4,700	House valued at	£10,500
Original capital	£2,000		
Capital payments to building society	£1,300	Representing total	
Appreciation since purchase	£2,500	'capital'	
	£10,500		£10,500

122

Trading and Profit and Loss Accounts

While a balance sheet shows us a picture of the company's financial state the trading and profit and loss accounts show us the activity in terms of sales, professional services or other input of money against the total cost of those activities. In those cases where the money input is by sales of goods we usually separate the trading, i.e. sales against purchases, from the profit and loss account, i.e. expenses against the difference of sales minus purchases.

Example of a trading account

Purchases	£8,000	Sales	£10,000
Gross profit c/d	£2,000		
	£10,000		£10,000

Profit and loss account

Wages	£1,000	Gross profit b/d	£2,000
Stationery	£50		
Heating	£20		
Miscellaneous	£10		
Net profit c/d	£920		
	£2,000		£2,000
		Net profit b/d	£920

This extremely simple example shows a net profit of £920. The trading account alone, shows £2000 profit (termed gross profit).

In the case of manufacturing companies there is usually a manufacturing account set out before the trading account, viz:

1 *Manufacturing account*

Materials	£3,000	Transfers to sales	
Wages	£14,000	(trading a/c)	£18,000
Transferred to P & L a/c	£1,000		
	£18,000		£18,000

2 *Trading account*

Transfers from factory	£18,000	Sales	£40,000
Transferred to P & L a/c	£22,000		
	£40,000		£40,000

3 *Profit and loss account*

Expenses	£13,000	Transferred from manufacturing a/c	£1,000
Net profit	£10,000	Transferred from trading a/c	£22,000
	£23,000		£23,000

In fact there can be several subdivisions of the profit and loss figures into various accounts. In this example the manufacturing account has contributed a profit at the previously agreed sales transfer of £18,000. Such subdivisions of the profit or loss total can help to identify the efficient parts of the total organisation.

The trading and profit and loss account example above is more applicable to the internal accounting in a company. The accounts prepared for external presentation have a different appearance. Before we deal with an example of this we define some standard terms.

Standard Terms we ought to know

Current assets These are assets which can be realised fairly easily. The three most commonest are:

> *Stock* The goods for sale, at cost price, but not the shelves they are on in the case of a shopkeeper.
>
> *Debtors* The money owing to the business for goods supplied or services rendered.
>
> *Cash* At bank, in hand or in quickly convertible amounts from suitable investments.

CURRENT LIABILITIES These are liabilities we have now as distinct from the future or longer term. They consist of items such as:

Provision for taxation due No explanation needed as to what this is.

Creditors The money the business owes for goods and services supplied to it, often split into trade creditors, i.e. for goods and services to be resold, and other creditors which may include items like fixtures and fittings the business has purchased but not yet paid for.

Bank overdraft Money borrowed for temporary financing.

Dividends Payments due to shareholders at the time.

Then there may be other items in a typical balance sheet, some of which can almost be deduced as being necessary from the terms above.

FIXED ASSETS These comprise items such as factories and other properties, fixtures and fittings, 'the shelves' in the shopkeeping example, plant and machinery and other such items.

LOANS These are normally loans to the business and thus would appear on the liabilities side. Any loans from the business would show on the asset side.

RESERVES This is a separate item in the balance sheet referring to investments or cash which are put away to cover new fixed assets or simply against a 'rainy day'.

DEPRECIATION In the case of some fixed assets there must be a lowering of the resale value as time passes. This may not be true of property but is certainly true of motor cars, lathes, factory equipment, etc. In each balance sheet this is allowed for by lowering the value by an amount of depreciation.

A Layout of a Company's Accounts

PROFIT AND LOSS ACCOUNT FOR THE YEAR
TO 31 DECEMBER 1971

	1971 £'000	1970 £'000
Turnover	37,000	31,000
Less cost of goods sold	34,000	28,500
Trading profit before taxation	3,000	2,500
Less taxation based on profits of the year	1,300	1,000
Profit after taxation	1,700	1,500
Appropriations proposed or made Dividends, gross		
Preference shares	100	100
Ordinary shares	1,300	1,200
	1,400	1,300
Profit retained	300	200
Total profit appropriated	1,700	1,500

With a profit and loss account should come an accompanying
sheet of explanations. This should include, particularly, details
of:

1 Cost of goods sold, including such items as:
> Expenditure on materials, supplies and services.
> Wages, salaries and pension payments.
> Depreciation.
> Interest.

2 Interest on borrowing, including:
> Bank overdrafts and advances.
> Loan stocks.
> Mortgages.

3 Directors emoluments, shareholdings and employees paid over
£10,000.

4 Taxation.

5 Shares on which dividends are to be paid.

BALANCE SHEET AS AT 31 DECEMBER 1971

	1971 £'000	1970 £'000	
Assets *less* liabilities			
Current assets			
Stock	9,000	8,500	
Debtors	11,000	10,000	
Cash	300	200	
	20,300	18,700	(i)
Less current liabilities			
Creditors and provisions	8,000	7,000	
Taxation	1,300	1,000	
Bank overdrafts	800	100	
Proposed final dividends	1,400	1,300	
	11,500	9,400	(ii)
Net current assets (i—ii)	8,800	9,300	
Fixed assets	14,000	13,000	
	22,800	22,300	
Financed by			
Loan stocks	2,700	2,700	
Loans	2,100	1,900	
Shares	9,000	9,000	
Reserves	9,000	8,700	
	22,800	22,300	

There should be an adequate explanation of the balance sheet like that of the profit and loss account. It would probably cover the following details.

1 Stock and work in progress. It should be stated how this has been valued and should normally be the lower of the approximate cost or net realisable value less any income for work in progress.
2 Debtors. Here there may be mention of any particularly large debtors.
3 Taxation. The provision for this may include liabilities of past years or changeable gains.
4 Details may be given in a different form to that in the profit and loss account of all stocks and shares issued, loans and bank overdrafts.
5 The reserves movement for the year should be stated. This may not be the simple addition of this year's allocation, but may include exceptional write-offs of stock, plant and development.
6 Details of fixed assets by type including additions, disposals and depreciation are necessary.
7 Finally commitments entered into but which cannot form part of the accounting should be stated. These may include capital items ordered or contingent liabilities, e.g. perhaps a condition of a recent purchase of another company may be to pay extra to the vendor in the event of profits being exceeded by a certain amount.

Management Ratios

In the running of any business there are obviously a great many facts and figures constantly being generated and updated, i.e. value of sales, amount of money owing to the business, amount of money owing to creditors, bank overdraft, stock, work in progress, etc.

It is useful to try to set down relationships between appropriate figures, e.g. in the simplest case and one about which most small shopkeepers are conscious, is the ratio of the amount of total purchases to average stock. This tells us how many times our stock is turned over in, say, a year. If we can increase the 'stock turn' then our business is generally healthier and more profitable. The extra profitability stems from not having money tied up in stock and/or increased sales.

Ratios should thus provide us with control information not only to help to optimise the running of the business, but to give warning of boundary conditions where the business may be in danger, e.g. overtrading or inability to pay debts. They also provide a basis for comparisons with other companies at home and overseas. This is in itself control information.

Types of Ratios

As one can guess, there are many opinions on what ratios are important and what the value of the ratio itself should be. There are, however, a few that seem to find most people on common ground.

LIQUIDITY RATIO

This is a sensitive barometer of a company's ability to meet its short-term commitments and is found by the ratio

$$\frac{\text{Liquid assets}}{\text{Current liabilities}}$$

By liquid assets we mean that part of the current assets which can be turned into cash within, say, 30 days. This includes cash in hand and at bank and any securities encashable in that time. It also includes good debtors who will or can be persuaded to pay in the time allowed.

Current liabilities are, as we have previously explained, with the exception of any bank overdraft facilities which has been promised for longer than the 30 days.

It is generally accepted that the ratio must be no lower than 1:1 while in special circumstances, e.g. slow debtor paying, it may have to be higher dependent mostly on the current ratio of creditors to debtors.

CURRENT RATIO

In the liquidity ratio case we were dealing with certain parts of the current assets and liabilities. In this ratio it is simply

$$\frac{\text{Current assets}}{\text{Current liabilities}}$$

The purpose of the ratio is to see whether the working capital available for operating the business is sufficient. The ratio should be in the 2:1 region, preferably higher, but should not be so high as to indicate the uneconomic use of capital.

SALES TO DEBTORS

This is an indicator of whether the credit control is adequate since it shows

$$\frac{\text{Sales}}{\text{Debtors}}$$

If control was set at 1 month for debtors then one would expect the ratio to be 12:1.

TURNOVER TO STAFF

This ratio is becoming more fashionable, i.e.

$$\frac{\text{Turnover}}{\text{Number of staff}}$$

and enables a measure of general comparison to be made with other companies in a similar business. The resulting figure for this ratio varies widely, but to a particular business it is important to know whether the overall effectiveness of its staff stands up to comparison.

SALES TO WORKING CAPITAL

This can give a warning to management when over-trading is present or likely to be.

OTHER RATIOS

There are many other ratios than can be listed, but our purpose here is only to create an awareness of the existence, need and usefulness of ratios by the examples above.

Operating Accounts

We said of the simple example earlier on manufacturing, trading and profit and loss accounts that this was more applicable inside the company. Most companies have their own layout for these, but a manager will be in contact regularly with operating accounts. It is after all the feedback to him of the performance in money terms of his department.

A manager requires information on the recent period of operation. This may be a month or four weeks or other period. He also requires an up to date total of the periods in this particular accounting year. All these operating accounts totalled across the company give a picture of the cash flow and relationship to the company budget.

sixteen Financial Choice

Introduction

In all types of management there are many decisions to be taken. A great majority are decisions that are reasonably easy to make based on the working principles of a particular company or from experience in a management post. Other decisions are more difficult, requiring the weighing of many facts, or more often, assumptions and estimates. Financial judgements play a large part in many of these decisions. It is obvious that the variety of questions will be almost infinite, but fortunately some guiding principles for financial choice can be written down.

Business consists of a continuous process of such choices. Shall we put our money into this or that project? Shall we buy this or that machine tool? Shall we achieve a task better by this or that method? There are several ways of evaluating the choices posed by such questions and although not all are effective if we take into account the erosion of the real value of money, it is necessary to remind ourselves of commonly used procedures. After this we will show more powerful and meaningful methods.

Payback

This is a simple method of looking at expenditure on a task or the purchase of a machine tool for example, and calculating the number of years over which the project will pay for itself. For example:

1 A machine tool costs £2000. It will enable economies in production of £400 per year to be made. The payback is 2000/400 = 5 years.

This is just a 'fact' and unless it can be compared to another similar but alternative purchase makes little real contribution in the matter of a financial choice. If we have two projects as in examples (2) and (3) below there is a greater point in considering the payback period.

2 The design and development of a new typewriter will cost £200,000. The estimated sales will provide profits of £15,000 the first year, £40,000 the second year, £60,000 the third year and £85,000 the fourth year. Payback period is 4 years. (Addition of yearly profits equals £200,000.)

3 A similar development costs £215,000 but no profit would be made the first year. The second year £10,000 profit is estimated, third year £40,000, fourth year £70,000, fifth year £70,000 and sixth year £25,000. Payback period is 6 years.

If we say that the payback time is the criterion for choosing one project from projects (2) and (3) then it would be (2).

However, suppose the choice is between completely dissimilar methods of achieving the same end result where the payback time is not really appropriate, e.g. a new underground railway costing £60m is likely to recover its cost in 8 years, the trains lasting about 20 years. The alternative is a fleet of new buses costing £9m, recovering the cost in 2 years and requiring new buses every 2 years. To say that the payback period of 2 years is shorter and therefore the buses should be used is plainly not a determining factor. Environmental, convenience and growth possibilities are but three other general considerations. Apart from these, in the sheer financial sense, although the payback period is shorter per purchase of buses, it is not immediately obvious from this that the bus solution is the most economic. Where comparisons can be made the payback term is a useful indication especially if the income or saving is likely to be cut off prematurely. Apart from this, the method does not present a clear and scientific answer for choosing one alternative from another.

Rate of Return (RR)

This assesses the return on capital as a percentage per annum of net return divided by capital, i.e. after allowing for depreciation. If the capital to initiate a project is £1000, income over 5 years is £450 per year, depreciation is 20 per cent of initial capital per year or £200, then net income per year therefore is £450−£200 = £250. Therefore:

$$\text{Rate of return} = 250/1000 \times 100 = 25 \text{ per cent}$$

This was an easy case to illustrate. What do we do if the income varies per year? Since it does not tell us much to have a different rate of return per year, about the only sensible solution is to total the various incomes and divide by the number of years. We thus have an average net income and can calculate an average RR. The capital too could vary in the sense that it may be injected at more than one time into the project. Averaging would again have to be done.

One of the worst features of RR is its inability to show clearly that the normal delay between capitalising the project and consequent income is affecting choices of projects. This initial delay could clearly affect the rate simply because no income is earned in the early years, but comparison of projects is difficult from the end figure as a further example will illustrate.

1 Project ABC: initial capital = £10,000.

Years	1	2	3	4	5
Income £	nil	nil	2,000	5,000	18,000
Less depreciation 20% per year	2,000	2,000	2,000	2,000	2,000
Net income	−2,000	−2,000	nil	3,000	16,000

Total net income = −£4000 + £19,000 = £15,000
Average net income = £3000 per year
RR = 3000/10,000 × 100 = 30 per cent

2 Project XYZ: initial capital = £10,000

Years	1	2	3	4	5
Income £	nil	3,000	5,000	9,000	8,000
Less depreciation 20% per year	2,000	2,000	2,000	2,000	2,000
Net income	−2,000	1,000	3,000	7,000	6,000

133

Total net income = $-£2000 + £17,000 = £15,000$
Average income = £3000 per year
RR = $3000/10,000 \times 100 = 30$ per cent

Thus we have the same rate of return in two projects where the cash flow is quite different. Which would you choose? It's a difficult choice but one factor that could influence us is that in project XYZ we get some real income in year 2, whereas in ABC we are still paying out in year 2 with no actual return until year 4. We obviously need some method that takes account of time as well as some form of rate of return.

Discounting Techniques

If you invest £100 in a building society you would expect the £100 to grow to £105 or so in 1 year's time because interest has been added. In the same way, if a debt of £100 is not paid to you until a year's time, the debt has not really been fully paid. You could have had £105 from the £100 if you had invested it so that £100 you receive in a year is only worth £x where £$x = 100/1 \cdot 05 \backsim £95 \cdot 2$ i.e. $95 \cdot 2 + 5/100 \times 95 \cdot 2 \backsim £100$.

This principle of valuing money that is to be received in the future so that we can compare the effects of different time delays and interest rates is called comparison of net present values or NPV. Closely allied to NPV is another method of taking time and cost of money into account called discounted cash flow (DCF).

If we buy a machine of any description that is capable of providing a means of revenue for some years then we can calculate a rate of interest we could pay for money borrowed to purchase the machine before the project becomes uneconomic. The method of calculating this and other forms of time/cost of money combinations is called discounted cash flow.

EXAMPLE 1

For an outlay of £950 which we borrow at 10 per cent interest on the reducing balance of the debt, we can buy a machine that saves £300 each year in production costs. How long will it take to get the £950 back? Interest is calculated at yearly intervals only. Taxation effects are excluded and the machine value for resale can be ignored. Firstly a table is constructed as below.

	Column 1	Column 2	Column 3	Column 4
Years	Initial or balance of capital to be paid back	Interest at 10%	Revenue savings from use of machine	Net balance Col. 1 + Col. 2 − Col. 3
1	950	95	300	745
2	745	75	300	520
3	520	52	300	272
4	272	27	300	−1

It can be seen that by adding 10 per cent interest to the reducing capital sum each year and taking into account the annual saving of £300, the project pays for itself in 4 years (ignoring the −£1 remainder). This means that the discounted cash flow interest value can be 10 per cent, to pay off in 4 years. If the remainder at 4 years had been a large negative value this would mean we had either over-succeeded in paying off in 4 years or we needed, say, 3 years instead to pay off. The 'over-succeeding' case is important because one of our criteria in financial choice may be to choose a number of years, say 4, in which projects have to pay off by the DCF method. If the balance in column 4 is a large enough negative value it means that a higher rate of interest than 10 per cent could be paid to borrow the £950 or that we make a profit of the percentage difference. We shall say more about this as we proceed with examples.

EXAMPLE 2

Calculate the DCF rate of return on the following project:

		£
1	Development costs, 1st year	25,000
2	Manufacturing unit costs, 2nd year	40,000
3	Sales revenue, 2nd year	10,000
4	Manufacturing unit costs, 3rd year	40,000
5	Sales revenue, 3rd year	80,000
6	Manufacturing unit costs, 4th year	40,000
7	Sales revenue, 4th year	80,000

Project closes at end of fourth year. Ignore taxation and any other complications.

This example is more difficult than the first because we are told the number of years the project is active and we have to find a

DCF percentage figure. Many trials could be made before we found the correct percentage which gave a zero (or near zero) balance at the end of the fifth year. We will lay out the figures vertically and choose easy percentage rates for a start, e.g. 10 and 20 per cent.

	Percentage rate	
	10%	20%
Development costs (initial capital, year 1)	£25,000	£25,000
+Interest year 1	2,500	5,000
	27,500	30,000
+Manufacturing costs, year 2	40,000	40,000
	67,500	70,000
−Sales income, year 2	10,000	10,000
	57,500	60,000
+Interest on outstanding capital, year 2	5,750	12,000
	63,250	72,000
+Manufacturing costs, year 3	40,000	40,000
	103,250	112,000
−Sales income, year 3	80,000	80,000
	23,250	32,000
+Interest on outstanding capital, year 3	2,325	6,400
	25,575	38,400
+Manufacturing costs, year 4	40,000	40,000
	65,575	78,400
−Sales income, year 4	80,000	80,000
	£−14,425	£−1,600

It is clear that due to the negative balance we could recover the costs on this project at a DCF rate slightly greater than 20 per cent. If the actual cost of borrowing money is 8 per cent we would make 12 per cent.

Now what we have done is inexact on several counts. We have:

1 Not bothered to go beyond 20 per cent to find the exact figure.
2 Shown interest payments for whole years whereas in years 2,

3 and 4 capital is flowing back during the year and thus the interest will not be exactly as shown.

3 Ignored taxation effects including grants and allowances.

To do better we have to do much more work and in many cases a judgement must be made as to whether the extra work is worth while. If large amounts are involved it will be necessary to repeat the calculations several times more to find the precise interest figure.

COMMENT 1

We can cut down the number of calculations in finding a DCF figure by using standard tables. If we remember what we are trying to do, i.e. to pay back all our capital using a rate of interest that results in a zero remainder then we can sum the *present values* of the revenue in, at the rate of interest such that this sum equals the original capital. Tables are available that give the present value of £1 at the end of any year from 1 to 50 years. For example £1 in 1 year's time at 10 per cent interest is equal to £1/1·1 now (its present value); £1 in 2 years' time is $1/(1·1)^2$ and so on. The value of $1/(1·1)^2$, etc, for 10 per cent and other percentages can be found in suitable tables.

This means that fairly quickly we can set down alternative percentage rates to find the correct one. Using Example 1 and tables we lay out this problem again, this time assuming we know the number of years but not the percentage. We try 8 and 12 per cent for a start.

Years	Net revenue	8% discount factors	DCFs at 8%	12% discount factors	DCFs at 12%
	Column 1	Column 2	Column 3	Column 4	Column 5
1	300	0·9259	278	0·8928	268
2	300	0·8573	257	0·7972	239
3	300	0·7938	238	0·7118	213
4	300	0·7350	220	0·6355	191
		Total	993	Total	911

If we subtract these totals from the original 950, then the 8 per cent gives −43 remainder and the 12 per cent +49. Thus from previous reasoning, 8 per cent is not enough because a negative remainder

137

occurs, and 12 per cent is too much because of a similar positive remainder. Interpolation (assuming the relationships are linear) gives approximately,

$$8\% + 43/92 \times (12\% - 8\%) = 9 \cdot 87$$
$$\simeq 10 \text{ per cent as before}$$

Another way of looking at the same problem is to split the capital and revenue and perform separate calculations based upon some rate of interest easy to apply, e.g. 10 per cent. The capital first has to be depreciated at 10 per cent. Using sinking fund tables we can find that to depreciate £950 at 10 per cent for 4 years we have to multiply $950 \times 0 \cdot 21547 = £204 \cdot 70$, i.e. this is the sum we must put away each year to provide 'new' capital, taking into account the compound interest of 10 per cent each year on the 'building up' amount.

The annual savings are £300 which, less depreciation of £204·70 leaves £95·3.

$$95 \cdot 3/950 \times 100 \text{ per cent} = 10 \text{ per cent (approximately) return on}$$
capital which is the result obtained in all three calculations

COMMENT 2

The question of interest payments shown only for a whole year can be answered by splitting the year into half years, quarters or even months and looking at the cash flows in those time periods. Obviously this multiplies the amount of work many times. If in doubt about the results on any example you have, take one more step (say into half years) and see what sort of result you then obtain. You must judge whether in your particular situation the differences are important.

COMMENT 3

The inclusion of taxation effects per project can generally be treated as revenue in or out for the appropriate year. The taxation rates can, of course, vary from year to year and one point to watch is the timing of such monies. It could be some time before refunds, for example, are paid into the business.

seventeen Value for Money

What is Value?

Value is a funny thing, it means so many different things to different people. Generally speaking people look at things or goods or services from several value viewpoints. How does the value of a piece of cake look, firstly from the eyes of a successful business-man who is slimming at that moment, and secondly to a starving refugee! If you happen to be on safari and lose the water bottle, what value a drink of water? The favourite picture in your wallet, what sentimental value do you place on it? You cut your finger, what value a piece of plaster to stop it bleeding? You have a punc-ture in your car one dark night, what value on your spare wheel, which you should carry? How do you value one washing machine from another? (Perhaps by buying a consumer magazine!)

All of these expressions of some sort of value can be grouped into four categories:

1 First, we have personal or sentimental values, such as a piece of jewellery, a kiddie's toy or a love letter. We wish to own these things, irrespective of value.
2 Second, we have a value of usefulness such as the piece of plaster or a starting handle when your car is bogged down in a ford and your battery won't work. A ride in a bumpy wagon may be better than a long walk!
3 Third, we have a value when we sell something. This is often an uncertain value. You could be very fortunate in that the old picture from the attic sells for £30,000. Most of us are

disappointed, however, especially when we try to sell our second-hand car.

4 The fourth value concerns the cost of goods and services, and this is where we as businessmen must pay our great attention.

Value for money does not mean everything has to be cheaper and does not always mean that costs are the only things we look at. What it does mean is that the value in any goods or services must be the highest that we can make it, i.e. *performance, quality and reliability at a cheaper cost to us or a better performance, quality and reliability at no extra cost or less than proportional extra cost.*

Another form of value we have not yet mentioned is that of contribution. Ultimately it will come to light in the guise of one of the other forms of value, but we like to think of it separately in order to measure it at source. How can we as managers do something practical about the value for money question? We need to know the areas where other people have successfully applied value for money techniques, often called value analysis.

Value Analysis

Value analysis is used as a general expression to cover activities over a very wide field. For example, one can analyse the maintenance service performed by the maintenance part of a company, the performance in a software house or the general performance of a manufacturing unit. Or it may more specifically be the analysis of value in products made by a manufacturing unit. The origin of value analysis is widely accepted to be from the activities of L. D. Miles working at General Electric (US) in about 1947. In mid-1949 he had a major article published in the *American Machinist*. In many US Government contracts the application of VA as a technique is obligatory.

Value Engineering

A further term that comes from value analysis is value engineering, which is the value analysis of engineering activities and engineering design and is an area where the greatest possible benefits can come from such an activity. It is here that the rest of the company activities are really decided. If the design is wrong, manu-

140

facturing may be expensive while the performance, quality and reliability aspect of the product make it difficult to sell.

The general method of attack to achieve the best value is once again planning for an achievement, this time by three rules:

1 *Set down clearly the function that is actually required of the goods or services.* What is it that is really wanted? This is not easy in some cases, but until this is done the next stage cannot be reached. Keep asking the question over and over again: What is it we really ought to be doing? What does the customer want? Is that compatible with what we can give him?

2 Only when we are sure we have defined the function can we then *establish the cost for the function or sub-functions by comparison with other similar functions, market knowledge, hypothesis or a combination of these and any other factors peculiar to the type of goods or services.*

3 *When this has been done you can then set to work to accomplish each function at that cost or less.* To do this you may have to generate the atmosphere, the enthusiasm, the knowledge and creativity.

In a sentence we must set our sights on what looks to be a difficult but achievable target in terms of cost for a given function and then get there.

It is important to realise this is not just a cost reduction process for this very rarely achieves the savings that value analysis does. The great difference is that VA looks at the function. If you take an example of a large company and a department within it, one manager may make cost reductions in a particular department by reducing the staff by 10 per cent. Another manager may look at the *function* of the department and realise the work could be done elsewhere in the company. He could thus (other things like personnel deployment allowing) close the department altogether. This is the difference.

Attitudes and Habits

These two traits of human nature can often rob a situation of much value. We are all guilty to a greater or lesser degree when it comes to something that upsets our set path. Habits work both for and against us. A habit like looking around properly when crossing the roads could be a life saver. A habit of not putting the

141

car handbrake on properly when stopping on a hill could be a disaster. Habits go with us in our work life and are reflected there whether we realise it or not. Unfortunately, habit can be stronger than reason and keep us in a sort of mental straitjacket.

Attitudes to change, often called road blocks, are listed in detail by specialists in the value field like Value Engineering Ltd. Some examples from their list are:

We can't take the chance.
It costs too much.
It's been tried before.
Let's think some more.
We can't fit it in.
We're making a profit now.
It's not our job.

The manager has to overcome these defects of habit and attitude such that he can get the maximum value out of the goods or services he is controlling. It means not accepting old values, and religiously applying the three rules of:

Examining the function.
Costing the function.
Obtaining the planned cost.

Manufacturing Example of Value Analysis

Value analysis in manufacturing has been widely exploited and in most companies there will be room for much saving. The British Productivity Council have said this about value:

'The Twenty Keys to Value
'Value Analysis is an organised approach to get the same performance at the lowest cost without affecting quality. Maximising product value, therefore, depends on the systematic appraisal of every product the company manufactures (to decide which products offer the greatest savings potential), followed by the formal application of the analytical process called Value Analysis.
'There are twenty rules which must be followed at all times if maximum product value is to be achieved, and these are:

1 Prepare a Value Analysis Programme for each product.
2 Apply creative thinking at all times.

3 Remove obstructions as they are met. Do not be deterred by 'roadblocks.'

4 Improve internal communications by example.

5 Bring new information into each area to be considered. Do not be content with custom and practice.

6 Get information from the best sources. Do not accept that the existing sources are necessarily the best.

7 Get all the facts. Be prepared for irrational answers to rational questions.

8 Evaluate each function separately.

9 Evaluate design by comparison.

10 Deal with the obvious first.

11 Know the manufacturing cost.

12 Put a £ sign on every tolerance.

13 Put a £ sign in every main idea.

14 Spend the company's money as you would your own.

15 Make full use of your company's services, facilities and resources.

16 Use standards whenever possible.

17 Use proprietary products whenever possible.

18 Use proprietary processes whenever possible.

19 Work on specific items; resist the temptation to generalise.

20 Use your own judgement; the judgement of others may be biased.

(Reproduced by courtesy of the British Productivity Council.)

The analytical process talked about is the practical method of achieving the results from the three rules we mentioned earlier. This is done by means of a job plan. It will or should not be the same method in every company, but an accepted one we have practised consists of seven stages.

1 THE SELECTION STAGE

This is the first and in some instances admittedly the most difficult stage. A product has to be chosen for the process of value analysis. Ideally the product should have a long production run, be of a fairly complex character and have a high cost × quantity figure. As is usual in the real world, there is not an ideal case and we have to make a judgement that a particular product will fit the bill. Simple arithmetic will reveal whether the anticipated cost of the VA exercise can be recovered by even a low return from the product quantity. Allowing for delays in implementation there is sufficient justification to proceed in the knowledge that many others have trod the same road with complete success. What the exercise costs is very dependent on the amount of effort, but if one man is full time and, say, five others are 5 per cent on it, then $1\frac{1}{4}$ average salaries plus overheads have to be recovered. It is expected that the cost of modifying the product will be covered by savings anyway. Returns of up to 80 per cent of the product cost have been listed by some companies. Returns of 20 to 30 per cent are common.

After the product has been chosen, the next stage, which is really the first part of the detailed analysis, can commence.

2 THE INFORMATION STAGE

This is where we analyse the function for costs, cost by sub-functions, specifications and market criteria so that we have a complete dossier on cost/functions. This work is usually done by the VA team leader with information from the specialist functions of the company.

3 THE SPECULATION STAGE

This can be done in several ways: the object is think and think again of ways of reducing the cost of functions. Brainstorming can be used, and we have personal experience of it. We consider it works excellently if a strong bond and will to communicate can be generated in the team sessions. Again we quote from the British Productivity Council:

'The speculation stage is that part of the analysis where brainstorming sessions can be used to the best advantage.
'The object of this is to arrive at alternative methods of achieving the same function. Exact cost information does not matter at this stage—ideas are more important.
'The sessions should aim at:
a Eliminating parts or assembly operations.
b Simplifying parts and assembly operations.
c Using standard parts in place of specially produced items.
d Simplifying design so that high speed manufacturing methods can be used. This could mean changing the material.
e Eliminating unnecessary finishing operations.
f Changing manufacturing tolerances to reduce machining time and scrap.

g Using cheaper alternative materials.

h Modifying parts to enable automatic assembly methods to be used.

i Substituting low cost processes for high.

j Using a higher cost material which, by virtue of its properties, permits of a simplified design being adopted thus resulting in a net saving.

k Buying finished parts more cheaply; perhaps by buying in larger quantities or by standardising on dimensions.

l Using alternative manufacturing methods, e.g. diecasting instead of forging.

m Using proprietary products in place of made-in parts.

n Using proprietary processes which may be less expensive than the low volume, internal processes at present employed.

o Using prefinished materials whenever possible, e.g. prepainted steel sheet.

'It is important that all ideas and possible alternatives be listed during the brainstorming session and that nothing be rejected at this stage. Subsequent evaluation will automatically eliminate many suggestions and time should not be spent, therefore, in judging the value of each suggestion. In any case, what appears at first to be ridiculous very often proves to be the ideal answer, after only minor development.'

(Reproduced by courtesy of the British Productivity Council.)

The main questions that help in the speculation stage are:

What is this part or assembly?
What does it do (function)?
What does it cost?
Can it be eliminated?
What else will do?

Brainstorming is not the only method of attacking the function at this stage, and indeed one of the problems is that the original designer may feel that all this apparent criticism is too much! This is where the VA team leader has to exercise great tact and persuasion to get everyone swinging along towards the common object.

Another way is for the VA engineer to sit with the engineers and others in turn and have what might be termed a 'confession session' where the question is continually asked 'Why did I do it this way?' We believe that brainstorming is more effective as we have personal experience of the almost brilliant results that can be

L

generated by a group of competent people building upon each others' ideas at one of the sessions.

EVALUATION AND PLANNING

It is now necessary to *evaluate* the ideas against costs in order to get the most promising ideas selected. There may be repercussions in testing and maintenance for example, and the evaluation moves into the *planning* stage where the finally chosen changes are presented in the proper form to comply with the company change system. After this comes the actual change procedures and monitoring of the results, usually several months later. In value analysis activities that we have been interested in we have been able to carry out overlapping exercises at the VA meetings, e.g. after speculation on item A we have moved to evaluation on item B, planning on item C and monitoring actual results on work carried out on item D many months earlier. The examples, some of which we helped to do, may prove interesting and encouraging to anyone who has doubts about the subject:

1 A small engineering company making a relatively simple device to hold some electronic circuit boards, automatically moving them through all positions for inspection purposes. Original cost of this was £5. After VA including new materials, part redesign and simpler finishes, cost reduced to £3.20, a saving of 36 per cent on the original cost.

2 Adjustable foot for an electrical equipment cabinet, original cost £1.80. New cost approximately £1, a saving of 44 per cent.

3 Computer printing device after VA, simplification of functions, new parts design, different finishes, elimination of one part. Original cost £1500, savings £250 or 16·6 per cent per printer.

4 Family of power supplies, average cost before VA of £175. With new methods of mounting sub-assemblies, removal of redundant labelling, new inter-cabling and terminations derived from informal VA sessions (not brainstorming) average savings of £17 per power supply were made. Since these supplies were used in many hundreds, a useful overall saving resulted.

5 A packaging example from the files of Airfix Plastics Ltd, of Sunbury-on-Thames, manufacturers of plastic trays, shows

another way that value analysis was set to work. A manufacturer spent £500 per week on disposable cartons. By examining the problem with Airfix Plastics a more economical scheme was worked out. It involved an initial capital outlay for 16,000 trays plus a washing plant. The total cost of this was £20,000. Even after allowing 10 per cent interest on the initial capital, in the first year alone there was a small saving and thereafter a considerable saving per year after maintenance and replacement costs.

"I DON'T THINK MUCH OF HIS NEW BUDGETTING METHOD"

part four Be in Front : Keep in Front

eighteen Project Management

Introduction

It is highly probable that most managers will become involved in a project either as a line or functional manager helping the project, as a key member of a project team or as a project manager. Projects may be defined as having a clear start and finish. Examples are the construction of a dam, the building of a motorway, a hotel construction project, a block of flats, a feed-the-refugees project or the implementation of a computer system; the list is endless. The common factor is that projects are normally quite specific and complete tasks, unlike the normal management task which continues to exist over, perhaps, many years. An example of a project can be taken from one of our very large hotel groups where a new motor hotel is treated as a project up to the time the hotel opens to the public. It then becomes the responsibility of a line manager to continue operation of the hotel and run its normal services. This recognises the quite different attributes demanded before and after opening. The project involves the pulling together of many skills and disciplines often having very tight time and resource constraints, and it is usual to appoint a manager whose sole task is to manage just one job and its demand for much tactical decision making. The size of projects also varies tremendously. A small construction or engineering project may cost only a few hundred pounds, while the Churchill Falls power project in Canada is likely to cost over $1000m by the time it is complete. Despite this wide diversity in size and type, we believe that all projects have a great deal in common.

The first common aspect is that all projects require some form of effective management devoted to that particular project. We call this man a project manager. His responsibility is to see the project through from its start to its completion and to ensure that it is a successful completion.

Why do we need Project Management?

Because a project is a complete task, of necessity it must require many skills and disciplines to effect a successful end result. This will mean in a typical situation many different departments and skills within a company and also, very likely, many subcontractors. There may also be other companies and specialists involved. In a very large company there may be literally hundreds of separate departments, many of them dealing with specialised aspects of the company's work. Each department generally has only limited contact with a few of the other departments in the company, and no contact at all with most of the other departments. The number of managerial interfaces grows alarmingly. You have only to consider that if 20 departments are involved in a project, if they each had to speak to one another it would result in 190 two-way communication links. This co-ordination difficulty often gives rise to the failure of one party to understand the involvement of the others, and very probably the failure of all parties to understand something from one essential document or requirement. A major source of uncertainty and confusion arises.

When a project manager is appointed he acts as a focal point for the project. He can make a coherent plan covering all the activities involved and make sure that everybody involved knows what their part in the plan is to be. From his overall knowledge of the project picture, he is able to appreciate any changes in the plan or timescale involving any one party.

An important aspect of project management is the question of the style of management which differs quite a lot from that of the normal line management. There is also to be considered the relationships between line or function managers and project managers. Often a project manager has no direct responsibility or authority over line managers; he has to get his project plans carried through from the authority deriving from the situation and from his powers of persuasion. A project manager who continually has to go to higher authority or senior management in order to bring pressure on line managers is very quickly going to become unpopular and in the end ineffective. There are many occasions where with goodwill he can persuade a line manager to do something which senior management would never be prepared to instruct the line manager to do. People are the centre of all management, but perhaps more especially so in project management.

The Key Techniques

In looking across the board at different projects, there are common points which have given rise to particular studies and the setting down of sensible guidelines. They are all based on good management disciplines and in our book *Successful Project Management* (Business Books Ltd) we have suggested that it is useful to consider seven key techniques (or guide lines) in order to thoroughly plan and manage a project. Like many other such guidelines once expressed they seem simple. Any difficulty, perhaps, is caused through carrying out less than thoroughly the suggested disciplines laid down.

1 Defining the Project

The first of the key techniques is to define the project. It does not require much imagination to believe that if we do not define what we are trying to do, we are unlikely to achieve it. In our experience, shared by many others in this field, a poor definition is often the first rock on which many an optimistic project has foundered. A whole series of questions must come to mind in trying to define a project. Take a relatively simple task of building a house or a bungalow. If you say to a builder 'Build me a house', what is he to do? He will want information on the type of house, size, number of rooms, what it must cost, what it must look like, where it is to be and a hundred and one other details ranging from size of rooms to the colour of the paint. The house has to be defined in detail. Even if you buy a house already finished, someone must have defined it before it was built. Out of the simple example we can pick certain issues that must pertain to other projects:

What are we trying to do?
In this case build a house.

What is the description of the project?
This is likely to consist of a simple description plus plans and specifications.

153

How much must it cost?
Will we find all the money, or will we need a mortgage?

How long will it take to build?

What resources will be required?
In this case we subcontract to the builder.

Are we getting the best value for money?

How must it perform?
This is a function of the design, the position of the house, the comfort of the rooms (with items like central heating and air conditioning improving the comfort).

How long must it last?
This is determined by the quality of the design and the quality and reliability of all the parts.

How can it be tested to see whether it performs properly?
Certainly parts of it can be tested and inspected as the house is built, like foundations and electrical and other services. The real test in this case will come from living in it for a few years.

How can it be maintained?
Not too difficult in the house example.

Other questions that are not necessarily brought out in such a simple case as building a house, although they might apply, are:

Is the project viable?
What new design work is wanted?
Do we need specialist advice and help?

Into definition must come a clear picture of the contractual responsibilities which will bring out such things as performance, cost and guarantees. Are these normal to the industry at that time? Are any new frontiers on the commercial front arising?

The object must be to continue to question, search and identify until we are satisfied that we have confidence that all the facts that are possible to possess at the time are available. We must identify all the key activities in the project.

154

Performance.
Specifications.
Costs.
Deliveries.
Safety.
Interfacing with other products.
Reliability.
Maintainability.

Also in the key activities will come knowledge of any technical barriers.

We must also identify the key decisions, for example:

Long-term delivery items to be ordered.
Tooling to be ordered.
Money at risk before contract (this sometimes has to happen in the real world).
Any money or resource commitment.

In identifying such aspects of the project work we must continue the search through experts, consultants, experience, writings and competitors until we have the planned measure of confidence.

While this is going on there will, of course, be written documentation of the project definition in terms of:

Descriptions or plans of the key events and decision points.
Lists.
Specifications of end items and of the whole.
Salient contractual points.
Specifications to enable the items to be tested properly so that we know the performance can be achieved, and for operational use there will have to be maintenance arrangements and documentation.

In defining the project we are also using the results from the other six key techniques, which are:

2 Resources.
3 Timescales.
4 Costs.
5 Quality and reliability.
6 Value optimisation.
7 Measurement and control.

We shall discuss these separately, but the remaining activity in the definition is to be prepared for change. The definition will not stand still.

REQUIREMENTS MAY CHANGE There may be a business take-over or a change of mind by the customer or circumstances. Whatever the reason we may have to change the definition.

TECHNOLOGY There may be a breakthrough and we are forced to investigate and/or use new methods, materials or items. Such changes can come about within our own company, through subcontractors, other companies or competitors.

THE PRIORITY MAY CHANGE Other projects may become more important and cause cutbacks in yours, or there may be too many projects and some may have to be cut out altogether.

THE BUSINESS SCENE Changes like those in the motor industry of safety belts, bumpers and exhaust fumes all cause definition changes in the motor car. Environment changes generally cause definition changes throughout industry.
We must be prepared!

2 Resources

Key technique 2 concerns itself with resources of all kinds and includes:

FINANCE

Requirements for finance must be known from estimates and budgets. The provision of finance may involve work on loans, advance payments and special overseas problems. The cost of finance has to be known and the means of recovering it. The risk of the project against the reward must be weighed to help the financial decision. In looking at this, alternative actions should be considered. The cash flow of the project needs to be stated including the time-scales, amounts and break-even points.

HUMAN EFFORT

This concerns the types of effort:

Physical, e.g. porters, labourers, carpenters, steelworkers, bricklayers, etc.

Mental, e.g. clerks, engineers, programmers, etc.
Male or female.
Supervisory effort.
Managerial effort.

MATERIALS AND EQUIPMENT

This ranges from raw material requirements to fully finished goods
and from consumable items like water, paper, oil, etc, to motors,
cranes, diggers, tools, etc.

SPACE

We may need:

Land on which to put new buildings or new arrangements
within new buildings.
Space to test something before sending to a customer.
Special rooms for special tests.
Rooms and offices for engineers and clerks.

SERVICES AND FACILITIES

These might well include:

Tea.
Gas, water, electricity, etc.
A new road, port or airfield.

In key technique 2 there is nearly always a battle of compromise
between what resources are desirable and those which can be
funded. Timescales are always too short and resources too few!
Spare resources are nearly always needed but nobody wants to pay
for them. These are all the problems which must be consciously
tackled under resources and, as far as is known at that stage, incorporated into the definition.

3 Timescales

Key technique 3 is closely bound to resources as immediately one
is changed it has an effect on the other. This interaction is true of
all the key techniques, but probably more immediately noticeable
between resources and timescales.

We have to formulate timescales for all activities in a project;
both to obtain resources, where there might be long delivery times

157

and to apply the resources. There will always be the conflict between being timely for the market place, customer or desire, against resource limitations, including cash, and design or ideas limitations. Sales lost early are rarely recovered in the later stages of selling a product and the cash flow is not so favourable. There is a great deal one can do on any project by studying extremely carefully all activity timescales and the logic of how these activities are best fitted together.

There are several ways of constructing and recording the information in order to have a master plan and then schedules of work, but whatever method is used the vital task is always to identify clearly at any time the *critical path*. The critical path is that path of activities through the project that will take less time than any other path.

There are two pitfalls to watch for in timescale constructions and consequent operation in the project. Optimism is a human weakness, so when estimates are received for activity times it is valuable either to know the man who is giving them and what his estimates are usually worth, or to double check until you are reasonably sure the estimate is valid. The other pitfall is to economise on low cost items on a critical path. This can easily be penny wise and pound foolish. If the critical path lengthens the project lengthens.

4 Quality and Reliability

While these words have been largely applied to the manufacturing industry they apply to all work, and here make up key technique 4. The quality and reliability of goods or services should not be a last minute thought but must be built into those goods and services from the start. This is not a philanthropic gesture for the consumer soon knows what goods or services to buy and buy again. Goods and services must be acceptable to a consumer at a price he is prepared to pay.

It is easy to think of the need for reliability in such ventures as space and air travel, where failure is usually disastrous for those involved. Reliability in weapons, motor cars, trains, etc, are all highly desirable. Reliability in the parts for spare part surgery is a very personal, essential wish for reliability. Moreover, we have all said rude things about the domestic items that refuse to work.

Quality is a little harder to define. It is concerned in an item with looking good without shoddiness, having a marketing appeal, performing properly as it was intended to do. The length of time it performs properly brings us back to reliability. Quality is certainly not concerned with gold plating everything—that would not improve the intrinsic quality of a bicycle. But if someone invented frictionless bearings for the wheels, that would be quality improvement.

The challenge with all quality and reliability is to achieve the necessary, acceptable standards at the lowest cost. It is fairly easy to achieve it with unlimited funds, but then the cost is so high that no one is going to buy the goods or services. Even with the best materials, best work and appearance, but without designed purpose there is nearly always failure.

5 Costs

Without complicating the issue too much it is a fact that *price minus cost equals profit*. This being so then to a large degree profit is within our grasp to control on a project, provided that we can control the cost. This is key technique 5. There will be two main facets in the costing process. If we are doing a project that is not producing a range of products as would occur in, say, designing, developing and producing a new bridge or a custom built house, then the project cost is the same as the product cost and we are concerned with how much it costs to produce the one end item. The less these costs, consistent with carrying out the specification, the more profit we shall make.

In the case of a project which is going to result in a range of products being produced, for example designing, developing and manufacturing a new typewriter, there will be two distinct cost divisions. One, and in the end likely to be the more important cost, is the cost of the typewriter itself, as this will dictate the profit we can make on our sale. The market place usually dictates the selling price and, therefore, the profit is directly affected by the cost. The other cost facet is the cost of the design and development which may be amortised over the quantity of typewriters being made or as in some large companies it may simply be written off into the company's design and development overheads, which ultimately are written off in the total profit of the company. The important thing is that extra money spent in the project cost, i.e. the design and development, may in fact mean a greater profit if the product cost can be reduced substantially. It is, therefore, necessary to know how these project charges are to be written off, how much we can afford to spend in order to reduce the project cost and so on. The exact mechanics are outside the scope of this book, but if we can begin to think about this subject clearly then we are halfway home to the right solution.

One cost aspect that is often neglected is the feedback of all costs to designers from day one. It seems very obvious when one starts to think about it: how can design A be compared to design B without knowledge of costs?

If we have a cost feedback system that is immediate and accurate, then we shall probably be pulling up by the boot straps all departments such as estimating, process planning, production engineering, value engineering, etc.

6 Value Optimisation

We have covered most of the principles concerning value analysis, as set out in Chapter 17, but we will summarise key technique 6 in three short sentences:

> We should not accept old values.
> We should take a new look at present functions.
> We should use a system of value control.

7 Measurement and Control

We now come to key technique 7. As far as a project is concerned unless there is a continuous monitoring, measuring, feedback and control of all the functions appertaining to the project there is little doubt that the project will be either ineffective or go on to disaster. A very appropriate analogy is a ship's voyage. In the beginning, the voyage is planned and charted; in other words there is a master plan and work schedules. Allowances are made for wind and tide; in other words certain risks, the key decisions have been identified. On the voyage there is a continual charting of the course and corrections made, if there is a deviation from the plan. This is precisely the same as should happen on the project. In the ship example, if the navigational checks are not carried out it is highly probable the ship will land on the rocks, and so will a project. *Without time to measure, assess and control there may be no more time.*

Planning

We have defined the general key techniques that make up the job of planning a project. In practical terms we can with advantage summarise our planning when we think of Rudyard Kipling's honest serving men:

> I keep six honest serving men
> They taught me all I knew
> Their names are what and why and when,
> and how and where and who.

We define *what* is to be done. We detail all the sub-tasks and activities, and so that we shall know what they cost we give each an account code for cost recording and control purposes. We have to say *who* will do *what* since all sub-tasks and activities must be someone's responsibility. Responsibility breeds the need for effectiveness and 'getting things done' and this is a prerequisite for project management success.

The *when* calls for a complete master plan of all activities from which working schedules can be created. The *where* covers those items like where to build, where to site, where to subcontract and where to test. *How* means how to do it technically, how to manage the job and how to reconcile time, resources and costs. We must use *why* as our constant source of advice: Why do it that way? Why does it cost that much? Why plan this way or that?

In planning we should take note of the levels of importance of various tasks. We must be clear which are our major base lines and technical barriers. Thus we might have, say, three levels, the top level of task being those where we have to succeed and there is no alternative. They are the major critical path items. For other items we may be able to prepare contingency plans in advance and for yet another level simple rescheduling may suffice. Finally, in planning, we should recognise that we live in a real and imperfect world. We shall have less than perfect specifications; we shall be called on to do the impossible; we shall have money at risk; there will be inadequate resources and uncertainty and change. Planning must take this into account. Typical problems are:

> The project importance is not defined.
> The plan shows apparently unachievable dates.
> The project seems to be ignored by functional managements.
> Planning is not for small projects!
> Working back to make times fit!

Being alert to the general problems of planning is more than halfway to success.

Progress and Control of a Project

There are three measures that will bring us the greatest chance of success in progressing and controlling the project. Firstly, we must have an adequate plan, secondly we must know how to be able to measure progress and thirdly we must know how to anticipate problems.

We have already discussed the planning aspect now we must decide how we are to measure the points of progress along the project path. This is not an easy task, especially in the technical projects where, say, the testing of a particular device may only give a certain confidence that the device is working correctly. Time may not permit inexhaustible testing of the device; in fact in some electronic devices it would be virtually impossible to 100 per cent test them as the time factor would be approaching infinity. If, however, we don't have sufficient confidence that we have reached a certain point in the project progress, then theoretically we must not proceed further. This is where the judgement of the project manager and his team really comes into its own. Very often there will be only partial confidence that a particular milestone has been reached and yet the need to press on is great. Only judgement and the use of normal decision techniques can give the answer.

The third aspect of progress is to endeavour by means of good planning, experience and good decisions to actually anticipate the arrival of new problems. We know there is no such thing as a crystal ball but with progress, sufficient knowledge and experience we can get near to success. The three constituents of progress that we are trying to anticipate are timescales, costs and performance.

TIMESCALES

By examining very carefully the critical path and near critical paths on the project we can learn a lot. By noticing the number of contingent events at any one milestone we can get a clue as to probable trouble areas. It is fairly evident that the chance of a problem arising increases as more and more items have to be completed at a certain point before another item can start, assuming we are in doubt about the progress of these items.

COSTS

We should have a planned budget and we can measure our costs against this budget. We may well need (in most companies we find this so) both an estimate of committed expenditure and an actual accounting return of expenditure. It is not often that the accounts are returned quickly enough especially in a large company with several locations, thus a committed amount estimated by the project manager is very useful. It is most important that the costs are measured against the planned progress as we can read quite wrong meanings into any of the cost conditions. For example, if we are underspent or behindhand with progress the actual cost is likely to be lower than anticipated and so we should actually spend money to try and get our progress right if this seems sensible to do. On the other hand, if we are over-spent and progress is ahead of schedule, this may not necessarily be a bad thing, unless our cash flow position is affected too adversely.

PERFORMANCE

Progress must be measured against performance of parts or units or large end items, and we must try to measure the success at these various milestones. It is rare to find the position quite clear: a judgement will have to be made as to whether to proceed further.

PROGRESS/COST RELATIONSHIP

In some way we must relate the progress against expenditure on the task. While completion of a project in a specified time is one of our most essential objectives we cannot do this regardless of costs. Equally, it is little use under-spending and thinking this is a virtue if in fact the project is running late. The main problem in relating progress and cost is that actual cost is clearly and easily measurable while progress is not so obviously quantifiable. There are two approaches to the problem. One is to split up the project tasks by time and cost such that one can say: When I have achieved this task, or sub-task, I have achieved, say, £10,000 worth of progress. If this is done throughout the project it is then possible to relate actual expenditure (real money) against the project achievement in the money terms we have allocated. It does not have to be money we use as a measure of progress, it could be simply units of progress.

In Figure 4 we have a typical budget/expenditure curve with time as the x axis. Apart from the vagaries of accounting we should finish up with two curves, one for budget, one for actual expenditure. However, as we have already pointed out, this does not give us any clue about the relationship with progress. If we now, as in Figure 5, have a similar curve, but with the x axis in terms of progress units or progress money packages, then at any time we can draw a vertical line representing progress in units or money packages and show the relationship between this and the actual

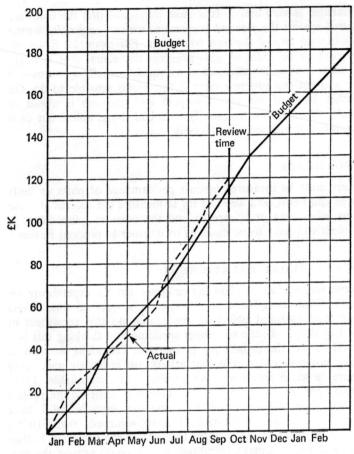

Fig.4

cost. This attempts to put the relationship in quantitive terms. From the picture emerging, one can make a judgement as to the effectiveness of the project. The problem under these conditions is that in most projects the work packages from which the units or money packages have been derived do not stay as neatly bundled as one would like. However, as long as our assessment of budget against work packages is done first, and then the actual expenditure and the line marking progress is put in afterwards, the measure can still be obtained.

The second method of relating costs and progress is merely to register progress on, say, a bar chart, register budget and expenditure on another chart and compare the two. The important item in each case is the accurate measurement of progress. Figure 6 shows a typical error in bar charting, where a number of activities are listed, a vertical line drawn as being the time of review of progress and the assumption made that the items on the left of the line are completed. You may well say that this is so simple that surely nobody would fall into such a trap.

We have seen many such examples. Figure 7 is one method of

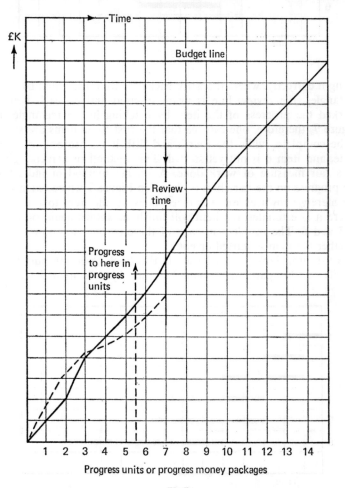

Fig.5

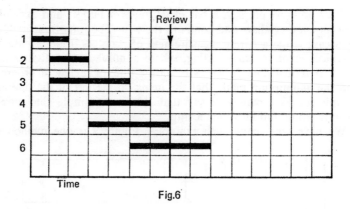

Fig.6

doing it correctly, where the work packages are represented by open rectangles, the review line is again inserted and on each item is marked the progress of the item by blacking in the rectangle. In Figure 7, therefore, one can see that the first three items are stated to be complete, while the fourth and fifth items are not yet complete, and item 6 is not yet started. This method of marking gives us a fair measure of work done. A further method of indicating the progress on the bar chart is shown in Figure 7 where extensions are merely shown as extra hatched lines on the item to the point where it is estimated the item will finish, as shown again on items 4, 5 and 6. The problem in each of these cases is to show clearly whether the item is started or not.

We do not think it appropriate in this book to go into any more details on this particular point, but the object is to make us all

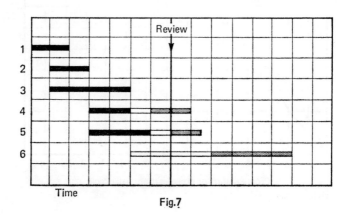

Fig.7

aware of the problem of cost and progress relationships, which is a key relationship in project management.

CHANGES

One of the worst offenders in upsetting progress and one we must control carefully is that of changes. These affect the three items we have discussed and a rigid change control system should be adopted from the start. In looking at changes we must pay particular attention to those which affect the base lines of the project, that is:

Performance.
Specification.
Costs.
Delivery.
Safety.
Interfacing.
Reliability.
Maintainability.

There will be others which will not have such a major effect. All changes have to be weighed both in an economic and general performance light and a system to evaluate, review and control changes is essential. Firstly there will be a change request for a particular change. Unless the nature of the change is so obvious as to occasion immediate rejection, which is rare, the change control body alerts all interested parties to the change and all comments are reviewed. If this does not reveal rejection at this stage, the change must be written by the appropriate body in the form of a detailed proposal so that unless it is rejected after this it is in a form whereby it could be implemented. If it is to be implemented the change control body must not only see this is done through the proper channels, but get a feedback from, say, manufacturing and field operations to support the original decisions.

The change control body may be a permanent feature of the company or it may be set up by the project office. The precise rules for whether or not a change is to be implemented in a particular project are of a tactical nature; they could not therefore be detailed here. However, general rules can be listed:

Omission from the original specification of the project. This has two connotations: can it be done in technical and timescale terms? Who is going to pay? If it is technically feasible, and the customer

167

will pay, in time (if necessary), and money, then the change may go through.

Omission to meet the specification. Similar to the above, except the contractor may have to pay. There may be more than one solution with different costs and time penalties.

Improvements to the specification. These require very careful consideration. They may be similar to the omissions case or they may be on that road to perfection the end of which, of course, we never reach.

nineteen Management Techniques

Unfortunately this expression has been put forward by so many people as the panacea of all effective management. We would like to say we certainly don't agree. Management techniques are exceedingly useful to know and indeed any one of them is the collection under one name of a series of disciplines that will help to solve a specific problem. As a manager we should certainly be aware of what management techniques are available because, even if we only use one or two of them successfully, it may well make us much more effective and improve our chances of getting or giving value for money. Having said that, however, we must never lose sight of the fact that 'good' management is still largely based on 'sound judgement', derived from common sense or logical thinking and experience. Even though the pace of science and technology continues to increase all the time, we are without crystal balls, so the need for judgement remains.

Actually, 'management techniques' is somewhat a misnomer, the word 'management' being the offender. Anyone can use them and indeed as many non-managers use them as managers. It is not our intention to fill this chapter with descriptions of all the management techniques available and we have already mentioned or described in other chapters the subjects of DCF and NPV, management by objectives (MBO), value analysis and management ratios. Two others with which we have also been closely associated are network analysis of timescales and brainstorming.

Network Analysis of Timescales
We start with this because it follows on from the previous chapter

169

on project management where the accurate estimation and control of timescales is essential. There are many publications on this subject and more working details are available, but in essence in timescale analysis we are concerned with:

The time an activity will probably take.
The time we would like it to take.
The time it actually takes.
The order of activities in relation to one another.
The 'estimates' of the critical and near critical paths through the project in timescale terms.

Note that at this stage we do not bring in separately the subject of resources and costs. These can be incorporated, but can also be kept distinct if desired. In the three time statements above the resources and costs are inherent in the definitions.

The items we have outlined above can be dealt with by several means, the most popular of which are bar charts, but we have no doubt that to avoid many problems of ambiguity and interrelationship a network must be constructed for initially planning a task. Management charts and working schedules on the other hand can be most effective by bar charts.

THE NETWORK

Firstly, it is a very simple device, requires only arithmetic, the same degree of knowledge of the task to be analysed as with any other method, but by its particular nature probably forces the manager to think more than with other methods. In forcing a better thinking process, it is then much more likely than the timescale plan to withstand the rigours of a typical project.

A network can be constructed for literally any task. If, say, we are considering the installation of a computer we could with advantage draw a network of the various activities. The simplest start would be to show the site and installation, but this is only a fraction of the problem and does not yet constitute a network. The activities are shown in Figure 8 as arrowed lines between the events, which are circled numbers; for example, 'define site' culminates in event 2 which could be called 'site defined'. This obviously must come before the activity called 'select site' and so on. If we add more activities a very small, simple network begins to appear. We could go on until we had added all the activities that should be included. This could easily be a hundred.

If activities are timed in, say, weeks, as in Figure 8 we can add

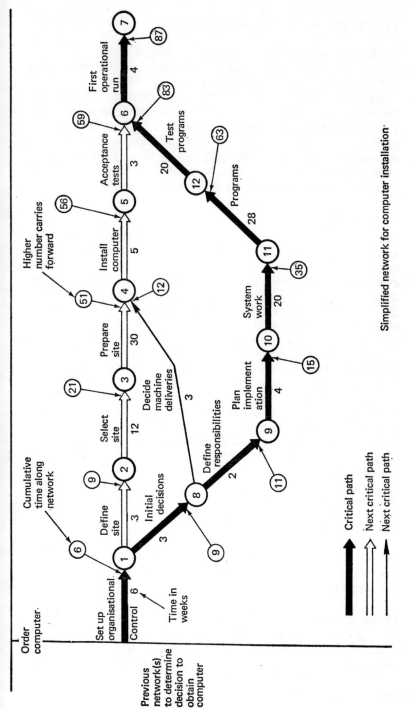

Fig.8

Simplified network for computer installation

up those activities that constitute the longest time. This is the critical path. Other routes will vary in total time from near equal to far removed from the critical path.

We have put some times against the activities and shaded heavily the critical path. The next critical path is double lined. The network is, of course, very incomplete and undetailed, but our purpose is only to illustrate the technique. From such a simple start we can see the time the task will probably take. If this is not the same as we would like it to take, we must re-examine the logic and times of all activities to see if a different arrangement will help.

Brainstorming

The experience of one of the authors is that brainstorming is an effective means of generating new ideas. In value analysis situations ideas have been forthcoming that seemed unlikely to have evolved under other circumstances. It is not an easy process in that the people have probably got to work together several times before the best results occur. The problem is that of defence against ideas, e.g. a discussion on a pet design of a designer member. In other words 'vested interests' is one of the real problems. Our experience is of about six to eight people working on design improvement ideas, but the technique can be used on virtually any problem. It is not particularly expensive to set up and probably the first difficult feature is to find a suitable leader who during the 'think' sessions must not allow criticism of any ideas, however outrageous they may appear, and must keep whipping up the enthusiasm and ideas generation of the participants. Ideas should be built on ideas until a novel solution appears.

Atmosphere is all important. In one group we had, the operation was of little use, simply because by chance, individuals could not and would not get on together at all. On all other occasions, about twenty in all, valuable ideas were forthcoming at these brainstorming meetings. It is a useful technique to try when rapid and unusual results are required. The evaluation of the ideas is more effective if it includes the brainstorming of 'What is wrong with the new idea?' If the idea comes out well from this, it is likely to be useful and effective.

The 80/20 Rule

This interesting rule is based upon several instances like the purchasing one where in most products it is found that 20 per cent of the purchased items constitute 80 per cent of the cost, or conversely that 80 per cent of the items only constitute 20 per cent of the cost. The rule is obviously not highly scientific, but whether the figures are from 75/25 to 85/15, there are numerous instances which support the rule in general. In stocks, for instance, it will usually be found that 80 per cent of the value is in 20 per cent of the contents of the store.

The advantage of recognising the rule is that maximum effort should go into that smaller part, i.e. the 20 per cent to give the greater reward. In purchasing, for example, the controls and checks should go into that 20 per cent of the higher value items knowing then that they are controlling 80 per cent of the total value. It is therefore worth identifying clearly the higher value items.

Other Techniques

There are many more working methods or techniques such as we list now. Many, if not all, are used at some time or another by the operations research profession which itself aims to approach problems in a scientific and quantified manner. The use of any of them requires care and appreciation of what one is trying to achieve and the likely advantage.

DECISION TREES

A network similar in some respects to a timescale network is drawn so that various logical possibilities are 'treed'. The possibilities are labelled with a probability of their coming to fruition together with the costs of the various routes usually brought to a net present value. By working further on the sums of probabilities the method can point the way to a probable course or indicate the risks under various circumstances.

SMOOTHING

There are various forms of smoothing employed to attempt to provide a more meaningful picture of a set of variables, e.g. weekly sales figures. These might swing quite violently week by week. By performing even the most simple act of continuously plotting the average of the cumulating weekly figure (moving average) we are likely to see trends more easily. There are more sophisticated types of smoothing, but the results in any case must always be viewed for what they are. What they are not is a magic answer to our problems. What they do is to help present a case but they always require interpretation.

LINEAR PROGRAMMING

When relationships between various quantities are linear, e.g. transport costs for 10 journeys equals £100 and 11 journeys cost £110 or costs of production against quantity follow a straight line graph, then this technique can be used to optimise a situation where there is a complex mixture of business activities pulling in different ways.

MODELS

In this sense the term has come to mean the dissection of a company's activities and putting them together in the form of a mathematical model so that variations can be inserted and the effect noted. For example, in the simplest terms,

$$\text{Profit} = \text{Sales} - \text{Costs}$$

If we break this down further we can have

$$\text{Profit} = \text{Sales (Volume} \times \text{Selling price)} - \text{Costs}$$

If we break down further, we may well finish up with a total equation of formidable size and complexity. A computer program could be employed to calculate the effects of varying different aspects of the models, e.g. sales down 10 per cent or certain costs up 3 per cent.

REGRESSION ANALYSIS

This is a mathematical method to simplify and analyse trends from large amounts of data and enable suitable curves to be drawn to show relationships.

SENSITIVITY TESTS

Such tests are a simplified aspect of financial modelling that all managers should use. It is a case of looking at the boundary conditions of any situation and asking the question 'What would be the result if, for instance my costs rose by 5 per cent or the sales increased by 30 per cent?'

Conclusion

There are many other techniques as well as those mentioned above which can be useful and in some situations essential. Every manager should at least seek out more knowledge on all of them in case they may prove useful to him.

twenty Computers as Helpmates

Why do Computers Concern Managers?

Within the next decade nearly every manager will be involved with computers. Computers will be the concern of every manager, not just the computer managers.

Despite all the horror stories—about £1,000,000 gas bills and so on—computers can be a great help to managers. However, to make use of their help, managers need to understand a little of what computers are and what computing is all about. Carefully planned and introduced computer projects greatly improve a company's performance. In this chapter we aim to introduce you to computers and to the important benefits they can bring to you and your company.

What is a Computer?

First let us consider what a computer is. The uninitiated tend to have extreme views on computers. To some they are a panacea. To them the arrival of the computer will solve all problems. At the other extreme the computer is seen as the most formidable weapon in the armoury of Big Brother. He will use the computer to keep us down. The truth, as usual, lies midway between. If you have seen a computer 'in the flesh' or on film or television, you will know that it is contained in a series of cabinets which are various shapes and sizes. These house a range of electronic and mechanical gadgetry. The essential physical parts of a computer are input and output units, arithmetic units, control units and store.

Computer Programs

Computer programs are the series of instructions which a computer follows, in order to complete a task. In their final form they consist of a string of instructions in coded form. Computer people refer to the physical pieces which make up the computer as hardware and the programs as software. When a manufacturer supplies a computer to a customer, he normally supplies certain basic programs with the computer. The user then writes certain additional programs to control the particular type of work which he wants to do. These are known variously as applications programs, applications software or user programs. A recent trend is for manufacturers and independent programming firms, known as software houses, to produce and sell or rent standardised applications programs for such work as payroll preparation or stock control.

What is so Special about Computers?

Basically a computer is special for two reasons. The first is its tremendous speeds. For instance an ICL 4–72 computer can add together two sixteen digit numbers in 1 millionth part of a second. Even a small computer such as an ICL 1901A can add two seven digit numbers in $28\frac{1}{2}$ millionths of a second. Similarly it can make decisions and print out results at very high speed. Because of this great speed computers can undertake highly complex calculations which previously would have been virtually impossible or would have taken years to complete.

The second special thing about a computer is that it does precisely as it is told. Nowadays, a common excuse given by businesses for mistakes in invoices and accounts is that the work has just been transferred to a computer. The implication is that the computer has made the mistake. This is just not true. The computer has done precisely what it has been told by the human being who has written the program controlling it. As computer people say 'Garbage in, garbage out.' In other words the results produced by a computer will be as good as the programs, written by a human being, and as accurate as the basic information which has been fed into it.

This implicit obedience of the computer gives rise to many of the difficulties which occur in using them, especially when they are used for the first time in an organisation. It makes it essential to feed accurate information to the computer and to give it very precise instructions, in the form of a program, to provide for every eventuality. Complex computer applications can involve 100,000 or more separate program steps dealing with tens of thousands of different possible conditions. Total obedience combined with the large information storage capacity of a computer permits fast and accurate recall of information, which has been deposited in the computer backing store.

Benefits of a Computer

Before considering how your own firm might make use of a computer, what are the benefits which can be obtained? These could be listed as:

1 *Up-to-date information.* A good computer system can give you really up-to-date information. The information can be digested by the computer and presented to management in the form that it requires. This permits management on the basis of facts and greatly reduces the element of hunch in management. It gives back to large organisations one of the great advantages of small ones, the rapid and accurate transmission of up-to-date information.

2 *Central recording of mass information.* So-called data banks can be built up on a central system. Thousands of millions of characters of information can be held in the backing store of a large computer. Thus, if required, the stock levels in a hundred different local depots could be recorded in a central computer and kept constantly up-dated. Information in a data bank can also be made widely available by the use of a network of remote terminals. The cost of such centralised information systems is justified by the fact that many, duly authorised, people can have access to the information. Examples are seat reservation systems and stock market information systems.

3 *Improved knowledge of working system.* To put any work onto a computer requires really detailed study of the system. This frequently discloses illogicalities and worse in the system used. It frequently also reveals to individual managers that the actual system in operation differs considerably from the theoretical system. In fact, there are many cases where the main benefit obtained from installing a small computer system has lain in the thorough rethink of the system in the stage of preparing for the computer.

N

4 *Routine decision making.* If decisions are made by clerks on a routine basis according to a simple set of rules, then these decisions can be made by computer without the possibility of human error.

5 *Flexibility.* If a computer system is seen in the broad context of the firm and is properly designed it will enable a firm to react quickly and effectively to events. For instance, the effects of changes in tax rates can be quickly established and decisions on price changes, etc, which may involve detailed calculations can be implemented very quickly.

Computer Shortcomings

We are very fortunate when we find any new development which has no drawbacks. The computer too has its shortcomings and these must be recognised if it is to be used, effectively. The main shortcomings or limitations are:

1 *Input of accurate information.* Remember 'Garbage in, garbage out.' A central problem in computing is to get information correctly into it. The bulk of information goes into a computer in the form of punched card or tape, from some form of coded document or directly via a keyboard. Elaborate precautions must be taken to see that the data input—information fed into the computer—is correct. Every letter, number or symbol must be in precisely the right relative place. Leaving blank spaces between numbers or omitting a full stop or comma can reduce the input information to meaningless rubbish so far as the computer is concerned.

Most input has to be prepared by a data preparation section equipped with machines for punching holes into cards or paper tape. The girls are given forms containing the information for the computer. The forms are designed so that the girls can follow a simple set of punching instructions. They sit at a keyboard and type in the information; which is then punched into cards or a paper tape. The tape and forms are taken by a second girl who types the information into a verifier at the same time as the verifier reads the first tape. The verifier compares the second typing with the first tape and locks up if there is a discrepancy. A supervisor inspects the discrepancy and a correcting entry is made. The verifier finally produces a corrected tape. A similar process is followed with punched cards. Although good punch girls can make 8000 or so key depressions an hour, data preparation is a costly, labour intensive business, which even with the care taken is prone to error. There is consequently a constant search both for improved means of input and for closed loop computer systems, where as much as possible of the information is kept permanently in the computer's backing store.

Although we have described the data preparation process at length, it goes without saying that it is essential for clear and accurate information to reach the data preparation section. Some of the information sent to data preparation sections has to be seen to be believed, for its sheer scruffy illegibility. Beyond the physical state of the information documents, there may be illogicalities such as a spare part being given a different name and part number by different departments of the company. This happens more often than might be imagined.

When information is first fed into a computer system a program is normally used to vet it, that is to check that it meets certain simple criteria. For instance, if you input details of new employees, it might put checks on the salary rates quoted. These might at the simplest check that the salary fell within the range £500 to £5000 a year. The computer would comment on anything outside this range. Checks of this sort help to show up gross errors.

2 *Recognition of patterns.* A computer finds it extremely difficult to deal with slight inaccuracies in information. A clerk recognises that Abel A. Smith of 1 LABURNAM AVE is the same person as A. S. SMITH of the same address or Abel. S. SMITH of 1 LABBURNAM AVE. Quite complicated programming is required to enable a computer to recognise this. Normally discrepancies of this sort lead to faults in the way the input is dealt with. This is why, when you find yourself addressed by a computer, they generally address you by a long serial number. Pattern recognition is a particular problem when information is collected from many different sources.

3 *The computer is limited to dealing with situations which the programmer has foreseen.* If he has designed an invoicing system which makes no provision for altering purchase tax rates and if the rates are changed, then no invoices can be produced till a change is made to the program. The programmer should have provided a table of purchase tax rates, which could be altered by simply inputting the new rates in a prearranged way. This is a very simple example, but the point is that some foresight must be used in designing and programming your computer system. A well designed system permits a considerable degre of flexibility.

179

4 *Computers mean change.* No organisation is ever quite the same after installing a computer. Hopefully they are more efficient, sometimes they are less efficient but certainly they are different in the way they work. Unless the introduction of a computer system is carefully planned, it can be faced with a lot of staff opposition because of the character, both actual and feared.

5 *It costs time and money to implement a computer scheme.* It takes a long time, starting from scratch, to design and implement a computer project. A large project in a new field, involving the purchase of equipment and construction of a building to house the computer can take 5 years or more to plan and implement. Where a firm decides on its first use for a computer and buys one, it is probably 2 to 3 years before it has a good working system. Not only time is needed but a lot of effort. This results in considerable cost. Hopefully, the benefits will in due course justify the cost. We will deal later on with the breakdown of costs. At this point the main thing to remember is that the implementation of computer systems is expensive and hence not to be undertaken lightly.

Computer Bureaux

We have talked so far as though the only possibility if you want to use computers is to buy or rent your own. In fact there are large numbers of computer bureaux. The services that they supply vary. Many of them specialise in providing a particular type of service for a particular type of firm. For instance stockbroking firms can get their portfolio work done by computer bureaux. Although a great deal of the preparatory work is done for you in such cases, there is still a lot of work to be done in supplying the necessary information to the bureau and in preparing the people in your own firm to use the system. Doing some fairly self-contained work on a computer bureau can often be a good introduction to computers for a firm with no previous experience in this field.

Why Use a Computer?

Having considered the benefits and shortcomings of computers, why should we use one? Many and various reasons are given. Some that we have heard are:

> To give the bank a modern electronic image.
> Because our chief competitor is getting one.

Because modern management needs it.

Mr X heard about them on a course.

Because our present accounting methods are hopelessly inefficient.

We believe that the following are good reasons for investigating the possibility of using a computer:

1 *Cost saving.* Conventionally many people think of this in terms of staff savings. This tends to be a trap for the unwary. Computers themselves need staff, highly skilled and costly staff at that. There may well be staff cost savings where large numbers of clerical staff are employed. However, a more fruitful area in which to look lies in the area of working capital. If accurate and really up-to-date information would enable you to reduce your working capital—stocks, work in progress and cash balance—then a computer may be able to help.

2 *Staff problems.* If you have a high volume of routine clerical work and have difficulty in obtaining and retaining staff to do it then there may be a case for a computer. A computer may also help with peak loads on clerical departments, for example the twice yearly share dividend work.

3 *To accomplish specific types of calculation.* If you have complex calculations which have to be done involving comparatively simple sums which have to be repeated a great many times, then a computer can help. This is particularly so where there are a large number of factors, which are interrelated and which vary in value.

4 *To provide a better customer service.* Quicker handling of inquiries and quicker provision of service is possible with a computer system.

5 *Expansion.* Where your present control system is at the limit of its capacity and you wish to expand your operations, the planned introduction of a computer may be the answer.

These give some idea of good reasons to consider a computer system. Computers are for any organisation a considerable expense and a comparatively long-term undertaking. A computer project should only be embarked on after a very careful appraisal of the use to which the computer will be put, the company's aims and long-term plans, and the real cost. A computer like everything else in management should show a satisfactory return on the capital employed in it. In other words, before you decide to go ahead with a computer, you need to be convinced that you will get value for money.

Computer Applications

The following brief summaries indicate areas where many com panies already use computers effectively:

1 *Invoicing and sales analysis.* This is an area very suitable for the computer. Orders can be processed rapidly and accurately. Invoices, warehouse instructions and customers' statements are all produced from the same set of information. The customer's credit status and the state of his account can be checked automatically before the computer gives instructions for the dispatch of the goods. Accurate and up-to-date analysis of sales can be produced as a by-product of the order processing and invoicing system. It is normally a comparatively simple aspect of a company's activities to put on a computer, and a rewarding one.

2 *Share register.* The maintenance of the share register of a company with numerous shareholders can usefully be done by computer. It permits rapid production of dividends and other documents for shareholders. It is a type of work which is quite suitable for a company to put out to a computer bureau.

3 *Stock control.* This is an area of considerable dispute in many companies. The marketing men want high stocks to provide good backing for the sales force, while the accountants lament the amount of capital tied up. A sound computerised system can both reduce capital employed and improve the stock availability position.

4 *Production control.* Production control by computer can help to optimise machine tool use, identify bottle necks and smooth production flows. It can provide the ability to react quickly and effectively to the changing demands of the market place.

5 *Computer aided design.* Much of the detailed work of producing an engineering design for a new and complex product can be done by computer much more quickly and with fewer errors than

182

the same work done by humans. It is quite common for a designer to do his work in collaboration with the computer, connected to the computer via a video terminal trying one possibility and then another in rapid succession, making use of the computer's power to store a great mass of data and its ability to do rapid calculation.

6 *Vehicle routing.* Many organisations face the transportation problem. How to cover a particular set of call points in the most economic way with salesmen, delivery or collection vans? Computer programs exist to do this in an optimum fashion. Many bureaux offer this service and it can show substantial savings. Local corporations have found it worthwhile to use such programs for the routing of their refuse collection vans. The same technique can be used for the siting of distribution depots.

7 *Project management.* Computer programs are available to assist in many aspects of project management, e.g. PERT and DCF.

We have listed these computer uses only to give you some starting points. In fact computers are used in thousands of different ways. To fill in your knowledge and keep up to date, take the technical computer magazines which give good coverage to computer applications and user experience.

Computer Costs

A computer, that is to say the hardware, may cost somewhere in the range of £50,000 to £1,000,000 +. However, this is neither the beginning nor the end of the computer cost. The costs may be divided into stages:

> Initial evaluation.
> Development.
> Running.
> Replacement.

Initial evaluation costs are the money you spend in finding out about computers, studying your own firm's needs and deciding whether it is feasible to use a computer to meet these needs. It is essential for a new computer user to go through this stage. Money spent on the feasibility study may well be justified by the improvements in the existing system, even if a decision is made that a computer is not justified.

In going through the initial evaluation stage outside help may well be needed. It may be obtained by going to a firm of consultants specialising in computer consultancy. It may be obtained by hiring a person or people outside the firm who have computer experience. In some ways this is the best way of doing things, provided that senior management also take a major part in the evaluation. Problems arise if you make a poor selection of your computer specialist. Serious long-term trouble can be bought in this way. Another alternative is to go to a reputable computer manufacturer such as ICL and seek their advice and guidance.

A minimum period for an initial evaluation is likely to be three months. It can well be longer. Costs are limited to salaries, travelling, expenses and course fees. If consultants are employed they are likely to charge about £50 a day for the services of one of their staff. For small firms the result of a feasibilty study may well be to go to a computer bureau rather than to buy a computer.

Development costs are a considerable part of the total cost of a computer project. They include the costs involved in the selection of the computer. The cost of the computer and other capital costs may be treated as a development item or spread over the life of the computer and charged as an annual running cost. The computer itself has to have a room to live in. For a computer of any size this will have a false raised floor to allow the cables connecting the various cabinets of the computer to be tidily out of the way. Some form of acoustic ceiling panelling may be desirable. The room will have to be air conditioned and some special arrangements may be needed in connection with the electricity supplies. Some additional equipment and furniture will be needed. For instance, data preparation equipment will be needed to prepare the input and perhaps a guillotine for slicing and trimming the printed output.

A major element of cost in the development stage is the staff costs involved in preparing for the computer. These include the cost of systems analysis and programming, and the cost of training other staff to use the system.

Running costs will include the spread cost of the computer hardware, that is rental or amortisation. The cost of maintenance of the hardware can be a significant item and is likely to vary between 2 and 5 per cent of the capital cost for each year of maintenance. The cost will be much heavier for a computer which works round the clock seven days a week. Operating staff are required to run the computer and data preparation girls to provide a data preparation service. In addition some systems analysts and programmers will be needed to keep the system going, to make any necessary changes and to improve and extend the system. There will also be significant stationery and 'media' costs. Computers can use a a great deal of paper. The 'media' are such things as punched cards, magnetic tapes and disc packs. The latter two can be a significant cost item particularly if hamhanded operators damage a number of disc packs as replacements cost about £150 each. The actual cost varies, of course, according to the type of disc and the manufacturer. In addition to these costs, normal budget costs such as rent, cleaning and power should be included.

Replacement costs need to be considered and planned for from the beginning of a project. Computers are still in a phase of rapid development. Although most modern computers will work satisfactorily for ten years or more, rapid advance may make them obsolescent in five to seven years. The replacement of the computer will involve expense, not only in the buying of the new hardware but also in some degree of reprogramming to make the programs suitable for the new computer and also to take advantage of any improved facilities which it offers. Any realistic costing of a computer project must make allowance for these expenses.

Systems Analysis

A system is a set of procedures linked together to perform a specific function. The systems analyst studies a system and defines it logically so that a programmer, working from this definition can simply and straightforwardly turn the procedures into program code.

A non-mechanised system is seldom well documented and is often very muddled. The systems analyst takes a fresh look at it in the context of the company's aims. He considers the output required from the system, e.g. invoices, the input available, e.g. sales dockets, and the procedures that are required to convert the input information into the output form required. It is important that the systems analyst really does take a fresh look at the system and question the reasons for everything that is done. An old trap is to try to take the existing manual system exactly as it stands and put it onto the computer. This tends to be both wasteful and difficult. It is far better to think it out afresh and take full advantage of the power and speed of the computer. Another trap is to submerge your organisation in printed computer output. It is better to allow the computer to make the routine decisions and only output detailed information where it is really needed, for instance to send to custo-

185

mers or as reports to management of exceptional situations which require their attention.

Batch Processing

This is the conventional method of running a computer system. The input is collected up in batches and fed into the computer, which sorts it into the same sequence as the main computer file against which the input information is to be processed. The processing is then done, the computer file updated and the results printed out. Because all the work is done sequentially after the input has been sorted, it is possible to use magnetic tape as the storage medium for the computer files. High density magnetic tapes, which are similar in principle to those used on an ordinary domestic tape recorder, can hold up to 20 million characters of information. When one tape has been read, it can be rewound and a second tape put in its place. In this way batch processing can make use of very large files of information. Where a significant number of items on the main computer file have to be assessed in a run it is cheaper to use batch processing. Typically a payroll or share dividend run makes use of every record on its main file and hence is best done by batch processing.

Batch processing is the most commonly found type of computer processing. It is generally the cheapest and requires less expensive equipment than does real time processing.

Real Time Processing

This is the other main class of computer processing. In such a system, instead of waiting to batch up input information, it is instead fed into the computer and processed as it is received. The results are provided by the computer in time for those results to influence the future course of events. For instance, much of the computer work in connection with the Moon shots is real time. Nearer home, if you go to the offices of the main airlines in London to reserve a seat on a plane for a flight, the clerk receiving your inquiry will probably consult a computer via a terminal on his desk. He will key your inquiry in and a few seconds later offer you a seat on a particular flight. On your confirmation that you wish to accept the offered seat, he will feed a firm booking into the computer. Most real time systems in practice are also 'on-line', that is to say they have remote terminals connected directly to the computer via Post Office lines.

Real time computer systems are more difficult to program and control than conventional batch processing systems. There are a number of reasons for this. Perhaps the most important is the problem of recovery from failure of the system. In a batch system it is possible to go back to a previously arranged restart point and continue processing at the cost of a small amount of lost time. In real time systems much more elaborate arrangements are required. This is because a large number of input messages may be in the computer in various stages of processing.

Conclusion

We have discussed the use of computers at some length because we believe they are an established part of the management scene. The manager who knows nothing about computers is increasingly at a disadvantage. The manager who understands how computers can be applied to his work has a powerful helpmate at his elbow.

A Glossary of Computer Terms

ALGOL   An acronym for ALGOrithmic Language, a standard high level programming language for use in writing programs for scientific and engineering work.

ANCILLARY EQUIPMENT   Equipment used in connection with a computer installation, but not directly linked to it. It includes items like paper tape punches and verifiers guillotines and bursters.

CENTRAL PROCESSING UNIT (CPU)   The computer's arithmetic and control units.

COBOL   An acronym for COmmon Business Oriented Language, a standard high level programming language for use in writing programs dealing with business problems. This is probably the most widely used of the higher level languages.

COMPILER   A software program, normally supplied by the manufacturer, which interprets a high level language program and automatically produces the equivalent program, written in machine code.

CONFIGURATION   The physical units making up a computer, consisting of CPU (see above), store and peripheral units.

CONSOLE   The computer console is the desk at which the operator sits to control the computer. It normally has a typewriter on it. The computer uses the typewriter to type out its reports to the operator, the computer log. It is also used for the operator

187

to type instructions into the computer. There are also a number of buttons or switches which the operator uses to communicate with the computer.

DATA COLLECTION The collection of information (data) for input into the computer. Data collection covers both manual collection and automatic collection by use of a device linked directly to a computer.

DATA BANK A very large file of information held on backing store units so that every piece of information is directly accessible to the computer. Real time systems generally require a data bank.

DEDICATED SYSTEM A computer system, hardware and software, which is dedicated to one particular purpose, e.g. the LACES system is dedicated to handling the paper work connected with movement of cargo through Heathrow airport.

EDP Electronic Data Processing, i.e. data processing by electronic machines. It is a term commonly applied to computer work.

FLOW CHART A diagram showing the linking of procedures in a graphic manner. Systems analysts produce flow charts as part of the brief from which programmers write their programs. Programmers own detailed descriptions of the programs, which they have written, should include detailed flow charts.

FORTRAN An acronym for FORmula TRANslation, a standard high level language for use in writing programs to solve scientific problems.

HARDWARE The physical pieces of machinery which make up the computer.

HIGH LEVEL LANGUAGE A programming language, which uses terms approximating to those in every day use, e.g. a standardised basic English or scientific and mathematical symbols.

IMIS Integrated Management Information Systems. In this concept a company has central data base holding all the information available about its operations. Managers can get management information from the system quickly and easily. An IMIS is difficult to set up and program and expensive to run. It is possible to come an expensive cropper in setting up an IMIS. The concept itself is sound.

k Computer men use k as shorthand for 000 (thousands), e.g. a 393k byte store is a store of 393,000 bytes.

LEO Lyons Electronic Office. LEO I was the first computer in the world to be used regularly for commercial work (November 1951), for the Lyons bakery cost accounting. The LEO

188

computer company originally a subsidiary of J. Lyons & Co. is now incorporated in ICL.

LIGHT PEN A device which is used to write directly on the face of a special VDU (see below) and thus communicate directly to a computer.

LOW LEVEL LANGUAGE A simple programming language directly related to machine language but easier to learn and use.

MACHINE LANGUAGE The language of the machine itself. This varies from computer to computer. Users do not program in machine language, but use either a high or low level language. The users program is subsequently translated into machine code by software compilers supplied by the manufacturer.

MILLISECOND One thousandth part of a second.

MICROSECOND One millionth part of a second.

MULTI-PROGRAMMING A method of running a computer which allows the computer to run two or more programs simultaneously.

NANOSECOND One 1000th part of a microsecond, i.e. 10^{-9} second.

OPERATING SYSTEM A software program normally supplied by the manufacturer which controls and monitors the operation of the computer system.

PACKAGE A program or suite (set) of programs designed and written to carry out a particular type of work, e.g. share registration work. It is available in a standard package from the manufacturer or from a bureau or software house.

PERIPHERAL EQUIPMENT Hardware forming part of a computer system directly connected to and controlled by the CPU (see above), e.g. paper tape reader, magnetic tape unit or line printer.

PL 1 An acronym for Programming Language 1, a standard high level programming language for use in writing both business and scientific programs.

PROGRAM A detailed set of instructions which tell the computer to execute a sequence of operations.

RANDOM ACCESS The ability to obtain access to any piece of information on a file directly without reading sequentially through the file. It is like putting your hand directly into the correct pigeon hole in a letter rack to obtain your own letters.

RESPONSE TIME The time which elapses between entering a real time system and obtaining a reply from the system. It is used as a measure of efficiency of real time systems.

SOFTWARE The programs which cause the computer hardware to operate.

TELEPROCESSING Processing data received from a remote terminal.

TIMESHARING A system which enables many users to share the use of a computer system. The users may have their own computer files and programs held by the computer and obtain access to them from their own computer terminal in parallel with other users, each with their own files and programs.

VISUAL DISPLAY UNIT (VDU) A terminal unit with a cathode ray tube (CRT) on which the computer can display information. The CRT is associated with a keyboard which enables the user to input information to the computer.

twenty-one Marketing

The Marketing Concept

What has marketing got to do with me you may ask? Haven't I got enough to do looking after my own side of things? This attitude is understandable but is not conducive to doing your job well. The theoretical justification for any company is that it is in business to make a profit. The marketing concept suggests that in the long run a company will only succeed in doing so if it satisfies the needs of the market.

Many companies centre their thoughts on what they can develop or produce. They work on the theory that if they can produce better and cheaper goods or services, they must be successful. They become very production oriented; the manufacturing director thumps home the lesson that if only the sales force can unload the steady stream of goods which his factories turn out he can optimise the factory loading, reduce idle time for factory machinery and people, thus producing goods at minimum cost. Unfortunately, his calculations go astray if the sales force cannot push the goods onto a waiting public. The public will only buy the goods if they are convinced that they need them. A pushing salesman may occasionally persuade someone to buy an item, which he doesn't really want. He certainly won't succeed in making a steady stream of such sales. Broadly, people only buy goods or services if they think they need them.

If research and development are concentrated on improving the product and on reducing cost, this is very rewarding in the short term but may not be so in the long term. Many potential market needs are recognised and met by companies outside the field concerned. The need for better lighting and a more convenient and less messy means of supplying it may have been recognised by the makers of oil lamps. No doubt they worked hard at improving the wick, making a smoother feed for the wick, developing globes of a more effective shape and so on. However, totally new companies grew up to supply cheap and clean electric light and power. These companies were based on developments made well outside the existing lighting lamp and oil supply companies.

The company which is marketing oriented tries to identify the needs, actual or potential, of the market. Having identified the needs it tries to satisfy them. We speak of actual or potential needs, because the customer may not clearly recognise his own needs. He may know that he wants better, cleaner lighting or warmer housing or more reliable personal transportation but have little clear idea of how the need may be met. The need may even be less well defined than that. The user may just recognise the irritating need to carry oil to his house to fill his lamps, or he may recognise the length of time it takes his wife to starch and iron his collars. In the latter case the need of the market was recognised by the growth of laundry service. However, the real market need was uncovered and exploited by the makers of nylon and similar artificial fibres. The drip dry shirt and other drip dry products not only satisfied the market needs but in the process caused severe problems for the laundry industry, which had set out to meet the need in a more obvious way.

It follows from this that the crucial step in the development of an idea into a new product or service lies not in the research laboratory but in identifying the market need. The successful company is imbued with the marketing approach. Market considerations impact upon every aspect of a company's activities. The same thing should also apply to nationalised industries and State corporations. We would also argue that it should apply to the work of local and central government departments. After all most governments claim to operate 'for the people'. To illustrate the marketing concept at work we will consider how it works in a manufacturing company.

Market Research

Marketing we have said starts with the identification of customer needs. This is done by market research. Most companies do some form of market research even if they do not always recognise it as such. At the one extreme, the managing director's wife may give him her views on the company's products from time to time. At the other extreme, and particularly in large consumer products companies, there may be a large market research department making use of a wide range of techniques to try to establish the needs of the market.

It is in fact possible to carry out quite effective market research with only a very small department. If a company is an existing one, it is already directly in touch with a number of outlets for its goods. The sales force can feed back their views. If necessary the company can carry out a special survey to obtain their views. If the business is to provide goods or services for consumers, as opposed to supplying goods or services to industry and commerce, the staff and their families are consumers as well as work people. Their views, where appropriate, can be obtained as part of the market research effort. In particular they can be asked to act as guinea pigs to try out new or improved products.

Market research can involve a study of government statistics. For instance a manufacturer of prams is interested in statistics relating to births and size of family and in government forecasts of future trends in this field. Similarly a number of commercial organisations may make forecasts and provide statistics which may be applied to market research for your company. Banks, serious newspapers and the trade press are possible starting points for facts and trends.

Elaborate questionnaires can be prepared and put to a typical cross-section of potential customers. We are all familiar with political polls and many people will remember how widely inaccurate most of the polls were in forecasting the results of the 1970 UK elections. Market research polls can be an easy way to spend a lot of money. The value of the research depends on a number of factors. First the questions themselves must be very carefully thought out and must be completely unambiguous. Then the cross-section must be carefully selected. The results of a sample of, say, 1000 people questioned will purport to represent the views of possibly many millions of people. If the sample is not truly representative of the population being researched then the final result will be proportionately inaccurate. The smaller the sample that is taken, the more important it is to ensure that there is no bias in it. A random sample is not one carelessly selected at random. It is one which as nearly as possible represents the population of which it forms a part.

Test marketing is another tool of market research, again particu-

o

larly in the consumer products field. A pilot production run is started with a new product, perhaps by selling the product in a limited geographical area. With simple capital equipment, early prototype models may be placed with existing customers. The object of the exercise in either case is to establish the market reaction to the new product. The result may be to modify the product, to put it into full production or even to withdraw it from the market.

Whatever method is adopted one thing is certain: the real needs of the market must be established. A firm may go on for years, even for decades, making a product, acknowledged to be the best of its kind. It may be content that market research is not necessary because its product is selling steadily and that is all the evidence that's needed. Perhaps another firm, possibly not even in the same line of business, may be alert to the needs of the market. That firm may come up with a product more nearly matched to the needs of the market than the product of the existing company. The result may well be a loss, temporary or permanent, of a significant part of the market. A case worth studying is that of the razor blade market and the rise of Wilkinson Sword and the stainless steel blade.

Product Planning

It is one thing to discover what the market need is. It is another to find the way to meet the need. New products and services may be developed directly as a result of market research, having revealed a need which is not currently being met. The product planning department may set down a product aim, based on such research, and work forward until it can produce a plan for the production of a new product which meets the requirement. Many large companies approach their new product design in this way. Others merely follow a policy of 'continuous improvement' of existing products. One of the most difficult aspects of product planning is to take the results of research work or the development of new techniques and see how they can be used to satisfy the needs of the market. Yet identifying this link may be vital to the survival of a company or even of a country. The United Kingdom, for instance, spends an unusually high proportion of its gross national product on research, yet does not appear to reap the full advantage of this in the market place. Much of the early research in the field of radar, computers, atomic power and jet engines was done in the UK. In some of these fields some of the most advanced research in the world is still being done in the UK. Yet the UK by no means dominates the market in these fields. The reason lies in the marketing gap. Many UK companies in these fields are slow to see the real needs of their customers. They are more concerned with seeking perfection than in making use of the current state of development to meet those customer needs.

The company which launches a good product, which meets the users' needs may well saturate the market and prevent the company with a far better product ever getting a decent share of the market because the better product is too slow getting to the market. It is also true that companies have slogged on developing and introducing an advanced product only to see a marketing conscious company come into the industry at a later stage in the game, adapt the ideas of the early birds more closely to the needs of the market and sweep the pool. Whatever form a product planning department takes and wherever it fits in the company hierarchy it has to remember that it only stays in business if its new products satisfy the needs of the market.

Advertising and Promotion

One aspect of marketing which everyone knows about is advertising and promotion. Promotion embraces all those plastic toys in the breakfast cereals and the super competitions which you can enter free, so long as you entry is accompanied by labels or carton tops from the product being promoted.

There are those who think that advertising will sell anything. This is just not so. Advertising will only sell if, basically, it is selling a product which meets a market need. The need does not have to be a tangible one. Much of the advertising we see today trades on our need for acceptance and for security.

Advertising must be informative, it must carry a positive message, even if the message is little more than a brand name and an associated picture of effectiveness. It does not pay to try to be too clever. People may never get beyond the negative part of the message in captions like 'Don't buy our booze because. . . .' They may miss the clever ending, which has the advertising agency in stitches. Similarly it is a golden rule never to mention your competitors in your advertisements. Why give them free publicity? Even knocking copy is helping in drawing their name to the attention of the public.

Choice of advertising media can be of critical importance. Common sense may tell one whether to advertise a pornographic novel in the *Church Times* or a highbrow novel in the *Daily Mirror*.

195

Day-to-day decisions on where to advertise can be more tricky. Simply one is trying to reach the maximum number of people, who might seriously consider buying your product, at the minimum cost per head. Evaluating the alternatives can be quite complicated and some advertising agencies use computers to help them.

Everybody naturally considers themselves to be experts in advertising. In some companies a senior manager vets the proposed advertising. He may consult some of his colleagues, his secretary and maybe even his wife. The final advertisement becomes an unfortunate compromise between the original professionally produced job and the amateur improvements on it. The proverb applies in this field as in many others: Don't own a dog and bark yourself.

Price

Price is one of the most important factors in marketing. The simple approach to pricing is to work out the costs and add a margin to cover overheads, risk and profit. If the sales manager says the price is too high for him to sell the product and that it must be reduced by 20 per cent, then the production manager points out that if he increases production by 50 per cent he can reduce costs and hence price by the required 20 per cent.

This is illustrative of the wrong way to fix prices. First, if your company makes several different products it is very difficult to establish the true costs. It is also difficult to establish what overheads are rightly attributable to this product. If the sales manager was right in thinking he could sell the original number at the lower price, he may well be unable to sell the higher number to which he has committed himself in order to obtain the low price.

The volume of sales of an item normally bears some relationship to the price. The demand for some items doesn't vary much according to price. An example is salt. You would probably use as much as you do now if the price were halved, doubled or even multiplied by ten. Economists describe such items as being subject to inelastic demand. Other items are very price sensitive, for instance the volume of sales of lemons varies with price. Economists assume that the buyer will, other things being equal, always buy his goods at the lowest possible price. This is in practice not always so because goods are generally different in some way or other, if only in the packaging. In addition buyers for one reason or another do not always buy the cheapest goods. The man who buys a Rolls-Royce car and the woman buying a dress from a fashion house are not looking for cheapness. Even in the industrial field a

MARKETING

buyer may rate reliability, good service or a good reputation more highly than cheapness.

Ideally the price should be decided on a marketing view of what is possible. Whereas the typical salesman likes to be able to offer the lowest price, the marketing man tries to produce a product which most closely fits the needs of the market. Also in setting the price he is more concerned with total profit from sales rather than with the highest volume of sales.

Commercial Policy

Closely linked with the question of price is that of commercial policy. Is the company going to deal directly with the end user or is there to be an intermediary? In consumer goods there may be wholesalers and retailers. For capital goods there may be agency arrangements. Where there are intermediaries a decision must be made on their reward. It must be adequate and there may be a case for making it sufficiently attractive for him to want to push your product at the expense of your competitors'.

What will the price cover? Will it include any element for instruction manuals or for after sales service? Is it better to have a higher price and spend more on advertising? Should there be any difference in the marketing of the product in different segments of the market? Should any customers be given preferential treatment? For instance, customers buying a high volume may be offered a discount. A tyre manufacturer may offer a preferential price to a motor car manufacturer not only because of the size of the order but also because of the advertising value of having his tyres fitted as original equipment. There is also the hope that when the tyres need replacing the owner of the car may be idle and buy straight replacements rather than shop around.

Distribution and Selling

Distribution and sales are the final stage of marketing and not as some people believe the whole of marketing. This is not to disparage sales. There is more to it than sending out fast talkers with a strong foot for putting in doors. Methods of distribution have to be decided on. If distribution is to be from depots, then those depots have to be sited to best advantage. Large modern companies use mathematical and computer techniques to help them make the decision. Sales managers are constantly exercised by the problem of how to cover the prospects effectively. How can pros-

197

pective customers be identified? How should sales territories be defined? Should they be on a geographical basis or divided in some other way, e.g. by particular classes of customer?

In sales as in other areas the 80/20 per cent rule applies. It is quite common for 80 per cent by value of orders to come from 20 per cent of customers. It is also quite common for 80 per cent of sales to be made by 20 per cent of the salesmen. These are, of course, generalisations but they contain more than an element of truth. Effective sales management examines this situation. It may be that some marginal customers are not worth retaining. They may cost more to sell to than they bring in. Similarly the profit on the business which some salesmen bring in may not justify their salary and expenses.

Public Relations

Every company is or should be concerned about its public image. The same should be true of nationalised industries, government departments and local authorities. A company which is well thought of finds it easier than others to retain the loyalty of its customers, to recruit staff and obtain cooperation from central government and local authorities. Above all a good reputation, resulting from good public relations, helps to produce repeat orders and new customers.

Good public relations are not just a matter for the PRO or some public relations firm. It is an area in which every manager and every employee can play an important part. People judge a company not first by its product or its advertising, but by the behaviour of its staff and especially by the behaviour of its managers. Wherever a manager formally meets someone outside the company, he is being judged as the representative of the company. This is true whether he is meeting a customer, a prospective customer, an applicant for a job, a supplier or a visitor from the local technical college or local authority. People also judge on casual meetings. If you see a stranger in the reception area, when no receptionist is about, ask if you can help. Do the same if you find a stranger looking lost in the office corridor.

It is surprising how far opinion is influenced by casual comments in unguarded moments. Be careful in the local pub or restaurant at lunch time not to disparage your company so that people can hear. The chief engineer may be a bumbling incompetent old idiot but you should avoid the temptation to say so in public.

Your Contribution

Your attitude should be more positive than just guarding against indiscretions. You should set out, without flamboyant over-emphasis to speak well of your company and its products, whenever the opportunity presents itself.

If you can see a market need, which you believe your company could fulfil, do something about it, if it is only to put a note down about it to your market research department or to your own manager. You may be told that your idea has been thought of many times before, but don't be discouraged. The man who doesn't make a move doesn't put a foot wrong. The manager who is going to make a contribution to his company takes a broad view and tries to see beyond the narrow confines of his own immediate job. Meeting the needs of the market is an essential for every successful company. It is vital for every manager in the company.

Marketing

We have written briefly about the various aspects of marketing because we feel that marketing lies at the heart of any successful company. Every manager should know something about marketing. In particular he should think about the needs of his company's customers and how they can be satisfied.

Reading List

Part One

P. DRUCKER, *The Effective Executive.* Heinemann, 1967.
WILLIAM J. REDDIN, *Managerial Effectiveness.* McGraw-Hill, 1970.
J. S. DUGDALE and JAMES BRODIE, *Fundamentals of Management.*

Part Two

LORD ROBENS, *Human Engineering.* Jonathan Cape, 1970.
A History of the TUC 1868–1968: A Pictorial Survey of a Social Revolution. TUC, 1968.
MARY PARKER FOLLETT, *Dynamic Administration.* Pitman, 1941.
H. FAYOL, *General and Industrial Administration.* Pitman, 1949.
R. M. CYERT and J. G. MARCH, *A Behavioral Theory of the Firm.* Prentice Hall, 1963.
A. K. RICE, *The Enterprise and its Environment.* Tavistock, 1963.
TOM LUPTON, *Management and the Social Sciences.* Penguin, 1971.
Edited by V. H. VROOM and E. L. DECI, *Management and Motivation.* Penguin, 1970.
ELTON MAYO, *The Human Problems of an Industrial Civilisation.* Macmillan, 1933.
L. J. PETER and R. HULL, *The Peter Principle*, Pan Books, 1970.

Part Three

BRITISH PRODUCTIVITY COUNCIL. *Studies in Value Analysis* from 1964 as available.
L. D. MILES, *Techniques of Value Analysis and Engineering.* McGraw-Hill.

201

READING LIST

L. E. ROCKLEY, *Finance for the Non-Accountant*. Business Books, 1970.

Papers as produced by Value Engineering Ltd.

MERRETT and SYKES, *Capital Budgeting and Company Finance*. Longmans, Green & Co.

Part Four

WATLING and TAYLOR, *Successful Project Management*. Business Books, 1970.

REPORT OF NATIONAL ECONOMIC DEVELOPMENT OFFICE WORKING PARTY. (Chairman Mr T. A. L. Paton), *Large Industrial Construction Sites*. HMSO, 1970.

S. H. WEARNE and M. T. CUNNINGHAM (Eds), *Problems and Efficiency in the Management of Engineering Projects*. 1966. Symposium of 5 papers and discussion. University of Manchester Institute of Science and Technology.

D. I. CLELAND and W. R. KING, *Systems Analysis and Project Management*. McGraw-Hill, 1968.

JOHN ARGENTI, *Management Techniques*, Allen and Unwin, 1969.

Computers in Business. Compiled by the NCC, published by the BBC, 1971.

LAURA TATHAM, *The Use of Computers for Profit*. McGraw-Hill, 1969.

F. J. M. LAVER, *Introducing Computers*. HMSO, 1965.

A. FLETCHER, *Computer Science for Management*. Business Books, 1967.

M. V. WILKES, *Time Sharing Computer Systems*. Macdonald, 1968.

Index

203

INDEX